CASE STUDIES IN EDUCATIONAL PSYCHOLOGY

FRANK D. ADAMS

ROUTLEDGEFALMER
NEW YORK AND LONDON
2001

Published in 2001 by
RoutledgeFalmer
29 West 35th Street
New York, NY 10001

Published in Great Britain by
RoutledgeFalmer
11 New Fetter Lane
London EC4P 4EE

RoutledgeFalmer is an imprint of the Taylor & Francis Group

10   9   8   7   6   5   4   3   2   1

Library of Congress Cataloging-in-Publication Data
Adams, Frank D.
    Case studies in educational psychology / by Frank D. Adams.
        p. cm. — (Source books on education ; v. 16)
    Includes bibliographical references (p.) and index.
    ISBN 0-8153-3724-8 — ISBN 0-8153-3725-6 (pbk.)
    1. Educational psychology—United States—Case studies.   2. Problem children—Education—United States—Case studies.   I. Title.   II. Source books on education (RoutledgeFalmer (Firm)) ; v. 16.

LB1051 .A249 2000
370.15—dc21   00-030733

Printed on acid-free, 250-year-life paper
Manufactured in the United States of America

The principal goal of education is to create men and women who are capable of doing new things, not simply of repeating what other generations have done.

—Adapted from Jean Piaget, "The Language and Thought of the Child"

Contents

Introduction

It has become almost commonplace for professors of educational theory and practice to use the case study format. The case study gives education students some of the atmosphere, energy, and feeling of the classroom. It is a learning experience for both students and professor.

For more than twelve years, I have used case studies similar to those presented in this book in the college courses I teach. I continue to learn from the students in my courses; each semester, they read and reflect on these cases, bringing to their analysis a vast array of experiences and backgrounds that contributes to a deeper understanding of the educational psychology theories. Had parents and students from the elementary and secondary schools not kindly related their stories to me and had the students in my courses not provided feedback and reflection, the case studies in this book would have been less complex and would have possessed less reality. The cases herein are representations of the lives of the students who were in classes I taught in elementary, junior high/middle, and senior high school over the course of twenty years. I was lucky to have encountered these wonderful people; each one enriched my life both as a teacher and as a citizen of the surrounding community.

I am convinced that the case study method is an appropriate pedagogical technique for teacher education programs. It is an active learning process for both students and the professor, because it requires the professor to be knowledgeable about theorists and demonstrate useful applications of theories using the case study as the vehicle, and it lets students relate to and process the information presented in the theories.

The case study gives both the professor and teacher an opportunity to use classroom events recorded from another perspective as another tool of instruction. The real world of the average classroom requires use of problem-solving, analysis, and decision-making abilities on a daily basis. Rarely do

Case Study 1
Miss Jaynes

Miss Jaynes, a first-grade teacher, moves about the class carefully as her students complete an afternoon handwriting assignment. Miss Jaynes is in the fourth month of her first year as a teacher; she is quite pleased with her first class.

Six-and-a-half-year-old Brent squirms in his chair as he takes his pencil in his left hand and begins to trace the outlines of the numbers 3, 6, and 9. His fingers redden as he grinds the pencil into the paper. His arm stiff, he attempts to make the rounded shapes of the numerals with short rigid strokes. The number 6 takes on the appearance of the capital letter G. His eyes darken with concern when he attempts to form another 6. His hand tightens around the pencil. His movement on the paper gets more deliberate and strained with a short, pressed motion as opposed to a fluid rounded stroke. After intently comparing the two attempts with a noticeable frown, Brent takes his eraser and furiously begins to erase both numbers, only to tear the weakened paper. His face clouded with anger, he yells, "I can't do this!" He throws his pencil down on the desk, folds his arms across his chest, and glares at the paper.

Miss Jaynes recognizes the tantrum. She moves quickly to Brent's side and spends ten to fifteen minutes comforting and reassuring him. Unfortunately for Miss Jaynes, this is the tenth time this week a tantrum has occurred. It is only Wednesday and yet Brent's outbursts make Miss Jaynes dread the rest of the week.

Miss Jaynes has had six conferences with Brent's parents; during each session, the mother adamantly defended Brent's actions while the father sat passively and offered no comments. When pressed for a response, the father countered, "You know how boys are!" She has sent five evaluations to the parents, with no responses. Miss Jaynes also has had several conferences with the school principal, Mrs. Downs.

Mrs. Downs is sympathetic; however, she does not consider Brent to be as much a problem as Miss Jaynes does. The school is too small to have a school psychologist. The school district has a psychologist who visits all of the schools every two weeks. With ten schools to visit, the school district's psychologist is far too busy to spend more than ten minutes in conversation with Miss Jaynes.

QUESTIONS

1. Does Brent have a problem?
2. What information should Miss Jaynes provide to the psychologist?
3. How should Miss Jaynes change her classroom instruction to adapt to Brent?
4. What information should Miss Jaynes provide to the parents? To the principal?

Case Study 2
Damien

Damien is an unusually small five-year-old-boy with blond hair and brown eyes. He arrives at school each morning with his step-mother and two smaller sisters, ages two and three. He runs to the clothes closet and throws his book bag in the general vicinity of his assigned space. Spinning around, he looks into the room and heads for the toy box. The teacher calls, "Damien, get out your crayons and books before you play!" She receives no response. Damien continues toward the toy box. With more authority in her voice, she repeats the directions. This time, Damien turns his head, smiles, and goes to his desk to get out his books.

On the way to his desk, Damien sees the circus wagon and climbs aboard. All of his anger, his comments, and his frustrations can be heard throughout the classroom. Putting his hands on both sides, he rocks forward and back with his whole body in order to move the wagon. The room was filled with the normal classroom sounds of children before Damien arrived; now, the classroom is focused on the grunts, moans, and frustration of Damien in the circus wagon. His face puckers up to register his frustration and anger.

He has focused the attention of the classroom on himself with the sounds and the loud noise of his jerking movements. Terri, a boy the same age and size as Damien, begins to move closer to the wagon. Damien stops jerking the wagon when Terri asks if he could get in. Damien changes places with Terri. Damien bends down and yells "All aboard" and begins to push the wagon. Setting a collision course for the toy box, he clinches his jaw and increases speed. When the wagon crashes into the toy box, he falls to his knees and slides to an abrupt stop with a yell. Damien looks at Terri's face, and then looks around the room to see who else has noticed. Terri begins to cry loudly. Seeing how upset Terri is, Damien turns and slowly begins to edge away from the wreckage.

Damien has been in the classroom for almost ten minutes. The teacher frowns, says good-bye to Damien's stepmother, and then turns to face the daily problem: "What will Damien do today?" Damien is taken to the time-out chair for five minutes. He flops himself in the chair and watches the teacher intently for almost thirty seconds. Damien turns the chair around with a scoot and begins to follow the outlines of the cement in the wall. He sits down on the floor in a slip-off-the-chair motion and begins tying his shoe-laces in knots. Damien puts his feet in front of himself, rolls over on his stomach, and looks under the chair.

The teacher has been in this classroom for almost ten years; she has developed a well-deserved relationship with the community. The teacher has had conversations with Damien's stepmother every morning since the first day of school; it is now the first of October and there doesn't seem to be any change in Damien's behavior. Various agencies have tested Damien, and they indicate that he is normal for his age. All indicate that he is easily distracted and moody with bursts of temper tantrums.

QUESTIONS

1. What is Damien's level of performance: cognitive, moral, and psychomotor?
2. How could Damien benefit from additional one-on-one assistance?
3. What should the teacher do to enhance Damien's learning within a classroom setting?
4. How could a behavior management plan benefit Damien?

Case Study 3
Lindsay

Lindsay is six years old, cute, verbal, and bright; she is a smaller mirror image of her mother in all respects. She slips into a chair at the reading table and opens the basal reader. Leaning over, she smiles and giggles and then speaks to the child next to her, Shelley. Shelley immediately sits up and opens her reader. Lindsay raises her hand enthusiastically to show that she wishes to read first. A grimace of disappointment briefly shadows her face when someone else is selected. Lindsay indicates, to no one in particular, that the reader lacks her skill and is boring the rest of the class. She puts her book flat on the table and rests her head in her hand while following along with her eyes. After repeating the process three more times, Lindsay's eyes light up and a smile crosses her face as she is chosen to read next. When reading aloud, Lindsay takes her right index finger and points to each word. Stopping only briefly to sound out the word "another," she finishes her paragraph and looks up at the teacher with a proud grin.

She knows that she is a very good reader, and she reminds Shelley of this fact. Lindsay also reminds all the children around her that she is a very good reader; they appear to ignore her. Lindsay stands up, bends a knee onto the chair, and sits. Keeping this position for less than a minute, Lindsay again moves and resumes her original posture.

Following the story, Lindsay listens intently and watches the facial expressions of the next two readers in her group; she looks away only when the third-graders go by in the hall on their way to recess. She reminds the other students around her to pay attention to the reading. The other students in her reading group chat with each other, continue to read silently, and ignore Lindsay.

The teacher, Mrs. Cline, begins a discussion of the story "Ira Stays Over" by asking, "Who has a favorite stuffed animal they sleep with?" Lindsay bounces around on her chair with her hand raised and fingers wiggling for added attention. Mrs. Cline calls on Lindsay and comments on her quick response to the question. Lindsay smiles and proceeds to describe her pet, Blue Bunny, in great detail. When she has finished with her description, she reminds the other children about how good the teacher thought it was; they ignore her. When Mrs. Cline asks for other responses, Lindsay's hand shoots up again. This time the teacher ignores Lindsay; there is soft laughter that seems to spread around the classroom. Lindsay's smile becomes a frown; she groans and immediately begins to sulk and withdraw.

Lindsay spends the rest of the day by herself. She speaks only when someone speaks to her; otherwise she remains silent. There are twenty-five students in her class. Mrs. Cline notices that Lindsay is quiet, finally. Mrs. Cline likes to see Lindsay working quietly; to her it means that Lindsay is not "bossing around" the other students. The events of the reading class are repeated in exactly the same sequence every morning; they have occurred over the past five weeks without fail. The majority of the class does not like Lindsay. There are several students with whom she can talk; however, she does not have a "best friend." She prefers this, as does the rest of the class.

QUESTIONS

1. How can Mrs. Cline help Lindsay develop more effective interpersonal skills?
2. Why does Lindsay have difficulty relating to the other children?
3. How could the curriculum be altered to help Lindsay develop more effective learning skills?
4. What are some effective methods for developing cooperative learning in this situation?

Case Study 4
Dana

Dana focuses her attention and intense energy on the paper totem pole being made in art class today. Each student is to create a face that will be placed with other students' faces, one on top of the other, to create a totem pole. Dana lifts three colors of paper, one at a time; she studies each carefully before choosing a red sheet for her creation. With her tongue between her teeth, she grasps her scissors and, with great effort and concentration, begins the task of cutting out her totem head. With slow and deliberate movements, she thoughtfully and forcefully keeps working without talking to any of the other children at the table.

When she finishes, Dana holds up a crudely cut circle and beams with pride. She quickly turns and watches Connie, the girl next to her, cutting her paper. Shaking her head, Dana reaches toward Connie and attempts to take both paper and scissors from the girl. The unappreciated attempt to help is met with a loud "STOP IT!" Dana draws back quickly with a quizzical expression. She continues to try to take Connie's paper. There is much grabbing, pushing, and noise made during the exchange. Both students are showing signs of stress.

With thirty students in the art class, the teacher finally intervenes and is met with, "Connie wasn't doing it right!" The teacher instructs Dana to finish her own project and leave Connie alone. Dana looks at Connie in a last attempt to help and informs Connie that her own face is going to be the best. Dana returns to her mask. In less than five minutes, the struggle begins again. The teacher frowns and intervenes again. The process repeats itself until the teacher moves Dana to a new location.

Dana repeats the process with Ruth Ann; the results are the same. The major difference is that Ruth Ann is more vocal than Connie was. Ruth Ann announces to the class that she does not appreciate Dana's help with her art project. The announcement does not prevent Dana from trying to help Ruth

Ann again and again. The yelling between Ruth Ann and Dana stops all activity. The teacher moves Dana to a table in a corner by herself. This does not prevent Dana from yelling instructions for her nearest neighbor, Gail. Gail and Dana begin to yell at each other.

Eventually, the teacher intervenes; she recognizes that Dana has made no progress since the conference last Friday with her, her parents, the principal, and her classroom teacher. Dana transferred to the school one month ago, and she does not appear to have made the transition well. After four different conferences, Dana is still as abrasive and combative as she was on the first day of school. The teacher looks at the clock and announces that the art period is over and they are to get ready to go back to their class.

QUESTIONS

1. What is Dana's level of performance: cognitive, moral, and psychomotor?
2. How should the teacher have dealt with Dana's helpfulness in a constructive way?
3. What should the teacher have done to help Dana?
4. How can the teacher help the other students in the classroom learn to develop cooperative learning attitudes?
5. How does the teacher assist students in providing positive responses to Dana's behavior?

Case Study 5
Bryan

James Snow was one of the language arts teachers at the junior high school. He described Bryan as a happy, energetic, physically mature, and outgoing seventh-grader. For the previous two grading periods, Bryan's grades were erratic in all of his subjects. Bryan had often pointed out with pride to other class members that he had achieved all of the letters in the grading scale. His grades ranged from A to D in both grading periods. During the last PTA meeting at school, Bryan's parents described his behaviors in the classroom, in the lunchroom, and on the school bus as being "just a teenage boy filled with many emotions and energies that he eventually will grow out of." It was impossible for Mr. Snow to convince Bryan's parents that he had specific behaviors that were not acceptable. They ignored all references to Bryan's aberrant behaviors and suggested that Mr. Snow would learn how "little boys" behave when he had taught in the school longer than two years. Bryan's parents were teachers at the local high school and were outspoken in their support for Bryan. The exchange had taken less than ten minutes, and after it Mr. Snow felt as frustrated as he had felt before the meeting. As he walked quietly to his car, he said to himself "Now what do I do with Bryan tomorrow?"

No one had disputed the fact that Bryan had a short attention span as it related to the seventh-grade curriculum. His attention span was unusually short unless he found something in the day's activities that he particularly liked. When Bryan liked something, he became unusually attentive and articulate; Mr. Snow had often described it as Bryan's "obsessive period." Unfortunately for Mr. Snow and the class, this period did not occur often. Usually, one would find Bryan staring out the window, or into blank space or harassing his nearest neighbor.

During the past two grading periods, Mr. Snow and Bryan had met in conferences almost on a daily basis; Bryan had always maintained that class assignments and homework were boring, useless, and a waste of his valuable time. Bryan often had taken punishment rather than do a class assignment or homework. Bryan and Mr. Snow had daily, weekly, and monthly battles over whose responsibility it was to keep Bryan entertained during his classes.

In a majority of the conflicts that Bryan had with teachers, staff, and administration, he meticulously pointed out what the rules were and how they were to be observed. From Bryan's perspective, the rules governed all of the students' behavior except his. He perceived himself as being special; after all, he had been told quite often that he was gifted and did belong in the gifted and talented class. He seemed to take great delight in trying to manipulate the rules of the class or the school to his own benefit.

Developing basic listening skills or critical thinking skills was not important to Bryan. He refused to do any of the exercises designed to develop these skills. No matter what the costs for refusal were, he would not do the exercises. He would remind all that he was a gifted student and did not need to develop these skills; he had them in sufficient supply.

Interpersonal skills were a disaster for Bryan. He had great difficulty keeping his hands, feet, and mouth to himself. On the playground, in the cafeteria, or in the hall, Bryan would pick fights and wrestle with any student smaller than he or with any other student he could intimidate. He particularly liked to tease and taunt smaller girls in primary school. His mother had tried to justify Bryan's problems with boys and girls in primary school; she had explained often that Bryan was an only child. She defiantly maintained that Bryan was trying to establish relationships with the younger children. No amount of conversation had convinced her or her husband that Bryan had been responsible for his own troubles.

Bryan's interest in girls was nonexistent; he never had a female friend on a casual basis. When working in groups, Bryan would work with the boys, and refused to work with any of the girls in the group or in the class. He often reminded the girls that he played football and was physically and intellectually superior to all of them. The girls in the class were intimidated by him to such a degree that they consciously sought ways to avoid him.

Mr. Snow frequently counted the days to the end of school; unfortunately, there were still four more grading periods to go.

QUESTIONS

1. How can the class structure be altered to help Bryan develop more positive interpersonal skills?
2. What strategy would you suggest for working with Bryan's parents?
3. What are the characteristics of a gifted and talented individual?
4. How can the curriculum be altered to provide more opportunities for Bryan to develop interests?

Case Study 6
David

At school, David cannot sit still for longer than two minutes. He has trouble finishing his work, and he is often out of his seat without his teacher's permission. He is impatient and frequently throws temper tantrums when things do not go his way. The other children seem to be somewhat afraid of David because he hits or pushes them. David, the middle child in his family, is seven years old. His older sister, Darlene, is ten, and his younger brother, Danny, is five. His father works in a factory, and his mother stays home to care for the family. The family physician told them that David would eventually grow out of the erratic behavior. His parents state that David has had this behavior from birth.

David seems to be of average intelligence, but he does have trouble with reading and writing. When he tries to write, his letters are of various heights and widths, with many extra squiggly lines. The words he writes often look as though he has written them backwards and upside-down. Many of his written words are spelled correctly, but the first letter of some words may be missing. Reading for him is slow and extremely painful. David cannot participate in the regular reading groups because he has trouble staying in the group. Too often during the reading group, he would wander off by himself only to return to ask if it was his turn to read. David cannot distinguish between a lowercase and an uppercase letter. Even when he writes his own name, the letters are either all uppercase or all lowercase. He begins a word with a capital letter only if all of the letters in the word are capitalized.

David's mother says that he has similar problems at home. He constantly fights with his younger brother and the children whom his mother baby-sits. David does better in a one-on-one situation than he does in a group. He is able to concentrate on such things like a favorite TV show or a video game for relatively short periods. His father states that no matter what the punishment, David cannot sit in a chair for longer than two minutes. When David and his father mow the lawn, David will not stay with his father longer than three to four minutes before he goes off to explore something else.

On the playground, David runs around until he is almost physically exhausted. When he is encouraged to participate in group games like kick ball or dodge ball, he rarely remains with the game long enough to know how the game is played. When one is playing individual board games with David, patience is mandatory. Quite often, he will abruptly leave the game; several minutes later he will return and ask to play again.

QUESTIONS

1. What is David's current level of functioning?
2. How can the curriculum be altered to help him develop longer periods of time-on-task?
3. What role should the paraprofessional have when working with David on a one-on-one basis?
4. What should the teacher do to encourage cooperation between the school and the home?

Case Study 7
Leslie Ann

Leslie Ann was an average student in the sixth grade. She worked hard to achieve B's and C's in her classes. Almost always, Leslie Ann looked like she just stepped out of a shower, a cleanly scrubbed youngster. Neither ugly nor pretty, Leslie Ann was ordinary in appearance. It was often said that she looked just like her father. She worked diligently in the classroom on each of the daily assignments; she always submitted projects and assignments before they were due. During class discussions, she listened attentively. For most of the class period, Leslie was almost invisible. When her teachers were asked to describe her, a majority of them found it difficult to do so. The teachers remembered her simply as being quiet and working hard to get average grades.

Margaret, Leslie Ann's sister, was three years older and in ninth grade. Margaret had been the top student in her classes since the first grade; she found academics easy. Margaret was the mirror image of her mother—pretty, witty, talented, and popular. At any of the parties or club meetings, Margaret was always the center of attention. Many of the other freshmen, older students, and adults enjoyed her companionship. Margaret and her mother had a close relationship and spent considerable time together.

During the Christmas holidays, the family inherited a large amount of money. Before the inheritance, they had lived in an upper-middle-class neighborhood. After the inheritance, the family moved into an exclusive neighborhood. The parents were professionals with careers that generally were unaffected by their recent accumulation of wealth. Margaret appeared to take the inheritance as she had dealt with other successful events in her life, very well, with a minimum of effects on her daily life and friends.

During the first week after the holidays, Leslie Ann was unusually moody in all of her classes, especially world history; Mr. Gorman consistently had been encouraging to her in his class. Mr. Gorman and Leslie Ann had maintained a good relationship for the first half of the year. As an advisor, he took extra time to encourage, monitor, and counsel the new sixth-graders; he tried to be available to listen to them. During the five years of his teaching career, he often had been commended for his positive contributions to his students.

Leslie Ann's mood appeared to change dramatically from Monday to Friday during the first week back from the holidays. On the following Monday, Mr. Gorman tried to talk with her, but she told him she did not want or need to talk to him. On Tuesday afternoon in the middle of English class, one of Leslie Ann's friends accused her of stealing a lipstick from her purse. An investigation by the assistant principal revealed that the lipstick was in Leslie Ann's jacket. Although Leslie Ann denied the accusations, she received three days of detention. On the following Monday, two girls reported to their homeroom teacher that they had seen Leslie Ann taking money from one of the girls' purse, and three other girls said they had seen Leslie Ann handling the purse before the money was discovered missing.

Leslie Ann denied all of the accusations. Frequently, her denial became wild, with verbal outbursts, shouting accusations, and even threats. Often, these outbursts were followed by tears. It appeared that she could turn her emotions on and off at will.

QUESTIONS

1. If you were Mr. Gorman, what would you do to help Leslie Ann with her interpersonal skills?
2. How can Mr. Gorman help Leslie Ann improve her classroom behavior?
3. What specific things would you suggest to Leslie Ann's friends during this period of time?
4. If the thefts had occurred during your class, what would you have done to locate the money?

Case Study 8
John Davis Holtz

John Davis Holtz is a sixteen-year-old eleventh-grade student. Mr. Gleason, the homeroom and social studies teacher, noticed that whereas Mr. Holtz always drove John Davis to school in the mornings, the boy rode the school bus in the afternoons. Mr. Holtz, who appeared to be argumentative, hostile, and domineering, stated often that it was the only "quality time" that he and his son could spend together. When John Davis entered Mr. Gleason's homeroom in the morning, Mr. Gleason consistently noticed that John Davis was aggressive and openly hostile. For most of the morning, John Davis would be a student who acted as if the world were against him. By lunch time, John Davis would begin to behave much more like himself. He behaved like a young man with many friends whom he enjoyed.

John Davis is a slender, fragile-looking adolescent boy who is less developed physically than a majority of his peers. His father is tall and well developed physically. Mr. Gleason knew that Tom Holtz had been a star athlete in football and track at the local university.

Several times during the past four months, Mr. Gleason has tried to talk with the father about the erratic and troublesome behavior of John Davis. Regardless of the comments, explanation, and expressions of significant concern about the behavior, Tom Holtz defiantly maintained that John Davis would grow out of the behavior and that Mr. Gleason should not worry about it. Conferences with John Davis about his behavior would echo the same comments proposed by the father. No conference with the mother had been of any benefit; the mother only repeated what the father had said. She often had stated emphatically that she could not and would not interfere with the established relationship between father and son.

Mr. Gleason had devised several projects and activities to help John Davis develop a positive self-image. On the athletic field, in the gym, in the hallway, or in the cafeteria, he would ask John Davis how the day is going and intently would listen to the response. For the past four months, it had appeared that the special attention and activities made slight improvements in his behavior. The principal, staff, and teachers often would praise John Davis for his positive behavior.

During this same period, John Davis had demonstrated consistently an aggressive desire to fight; he had wanted to fight, verbally and/or physically, anyone and everyone for any minor irritation. This aggressiveness had caused John Davis many problems that resulted in conferences with Mr. Gleason, the school counselor, other teachers, the principal, and Tom Holtz. John Davis had received suspensions from activities, from classes, and from school. The father had been outspoken in his opposition of the decisions made by the school principal, the superintendent, or the school board. Tom Holtz believed that his son must "stand up for his rights or other people would walk all over him" and that the school was interfering with his normal development.

During the Thanksgiving holiday, John Davis's mother had to have surgery and was hospitalized for several weeks. On Monday when John Davis returned from the holiday period, he was unusually moody, could not sit in his chair long, talked to himself, and was aggressive toward the other students. On Thursday morning shortly after his father had left, John Davis began crying. He and Mr. Gleason were able to talk for almost thirty minutes. From the conversation Mr. Gleason got the general impression that John Davis wanted to run away from home and never return.

QUESTIONS

1. If you were Mr. Gleason, how would you respond to John Davis's classroom behavior?
2. Describe John Davis's current level of behavior?
3. How can the members of the class help John Davis?
4. How can problems similar to those described be handled within a classroom setting?

Case Study 10
Mrs. Lair and Her Daughters

Mrs. Brenda Lair had taught the fifth grade at Wilson Elementary School for the past ten years. Since her husband had died from a heart attack three years ago, she had managed to provide for herself and two daughters without any outside assistance. All of her friends and neighbors said that she had a difficult time; all of the events of her life appeared to have changed her dramatically. The community, the students, and parents believed that she was a good teacher; she operated a conservative and disciplined classroom. The students in her classes consistently scored extremely high on the school district's annual standardized tests.

At the beginning of the school year, Mrs. Lair transferred her two daughters from the school they were attending to Wilson Elementary. The primary reason that she gave to the principal was that her girls were not being properly supervised at the previous school. Jo Ann, who was nine and in the forth grade, and Barbara, who was twelve and in the sixth grade, had been in the gifted and talented classes for only one year. The girls had been admitted to the program at the same time and spent a great deal of time working and playing together in this class.

Since the fourth grade was on the same hall that she taught, Mrs. Lair asked Jo Ann's teacher, Mrs. Gold, to keep her informed if Jo Ann misbehaved in any way. Two days after Mrs. Lair had talked to Mrs. Gold, Jo Ann and two other girls were running in the hall going out to recess. Mrs. Gold made all three girls sit on the wall during recess rather than allowing them to play with the other students. When Mrs. Lair saw Jo Ann sitting on the wall, she immediately left her classroom, walked to Mrs. Gold, and was very vocal in her criticism of Mrs. Gold's discipline practice with Jo Ann. Everyone on the playground stopped and watched Mrs. Lair rant and rave for almost five minutes. At that point, Mrs. Gold told her class that recess was over and she left Mrs. Lair standing on the playground. During Mrs. Gold's planning period, she talked with the principal and explained Mrs. Lair's outburst. From the first week until the first grading period, Mrs. Gold received phone calls at home, memos, and letters from Mrs. Lair stating all of the things that she had done wrong that week.

The sixth grade was on the floor above the fourth and fifth grades. On the first day of school, Mrs. Lair asked Barbara's teacher, Mr. Hanney, to keep her informed if Barbara misbehaved in any way. Mr. Hanney explained that his philosophy of discipline stressed that students assume responsibility for their own actions. He assured Mrs. Lair that if there were any serious problems he would tell her. Mrs. Lair insisted that she be informed of her daughter's activities on a daily basis. Mr. Hanney did not respond to Mrs. Lair; he walked away. At the earliest opportunity, he informed the principal of what Mrs. Lair had told him. One week later, Mr. Hanney caught Barbara and another girl leaning out of a window and throwing paper wads at the students on the walkway. As part of the discipline, Barbara and the other girl had to remain in the study hall while the rest of the class went out for the afternoon recess. When Mrs. Lair discovered what had happened, she immediately confronted Mr. Hanney in front of the door of his classroom before the beginning of the recess period. She loudly criticized his handling of the situation and demanded an apology. Mr. Hanney suggested that they meet with the principal at a more appropriate time. Mrs. Lair refused and said that she would take the matter to the board of education. From the first week until the first grading period, Mr. Hanney received phone calls at home, memos, and letters from Mrs. Lair stating all of the things that he had done wrong that week.

Mrs. Lair did not stop writing memos and letters and telephoning the teachers; she also included the principal, the superintendent, and selected members of the board of education. The superintendent condensed the letters and provided the principal a weekly summary of Mrs. Lair's actions. It appeared that no one was happy and things were not improving with time.

Mrs. Gold submitted her grades and mentioned to the principal that Jo Ann had received C's and D's for her first grading period. Mrs. Gold wanted the principal to tell her what to do about Jo Ann's grades. Mr. Hanney submitted his grades and mentioned to the principal that Barbara had received F's in all of her subjects for the first grading period. Mr. Hanney wanted to know what to tell Mrs. Lair.

As the end of the first grading period neared, the girls' records arrived from the previous school. The principal kept the files until all of the girls' grades had been recorded. Before the grade reports were sent out, the principal held a conference with Mrs. Lair. It was not an experience that she or the principal anticipated. The records from the previous school had confirmed what that school had experienced during the first grading period. Both girls had maintained a D average and were constant discipline problems; the mother had been as much a discipline problem as the girls had been.

Case Study 12
Lynn

Teachers described Lynn as a survivor. Lynn's mother remarried shortly after Lynn's seventh birthday. When Lynn was ten years old, her mother left her with her stepfather and began living with another man in another state. Her mother never said good-bye to Lynn; she told the stepfather to tell her good-bye. For the past two years, her mother had not tried to communicate with Lynn.

As Lynn was entering the seventh grade, her stepfather remarried. Her stepmother had a daughter, Mary Kate, who was seven years old. The summer before seventh grade had been a period of tremendous change; the world that Lynn had known ended. The stepfather and Lynn had moved into the stepmother's house. Now, Lynn lived in a house with two strangers; she had left the friends in her neighborhood. Up to this point, she had been the "woman" of the house, with her own bedroom. She now shared a bedroom with Mary Kate; it was not the best arrangement for either girl.

August and September of the seventh grade came and went with only minor problems for the newly formed family; Mary Kate's birthday had been a major event, with many people involved. Lynn had met several girls and boys in the neighborhood and she developed two new best friends. She had tried to adjust to the new family arrangement, for she liked her stepfather very much. He was the only family she had, she thought.

Lynn was a good student. She found learning, studying, and writing to be fun and enjoyable. From first to sixth grade, she had always been one of the top students in her classes. At the beginning of this school year, the move to the new house meant that she had had to change schools. The beginning of school had been a stressful period for Lynn. Yet she saw it as a chance to make new friends; therefore, she began to study hard for her classes. Quickly, she became popular at the new school with her classmates as well as her teachers.

On October 1st, the day before Lynn's birthday, her stepmother told her that they could not afford a big birthday party for her. Instead of a party, her stepmother gave her a card and wished her a happy birthday. The next day at school, Mary Kate told her teachers that Lynn was not her sister but someone whom her family let live with them. By Monday of the following week, the school knew the story that Mary Kate had told. Before school began, Mrs. Watts, Lynn's homeroom teacher, asked if she could talk to Lynn.

QUESTIONS

1. What is Lynn's current level of functioning?
2. If you were Lynn's homeroom teacher, what would you say to Lynn?
3. As one of Lynn's teachers, how would you help Lynn to adjust to this new situation?
4. What would you say to Lynn's stepmother?

Case Study 13
Rene

Rene is fourteen years old and in the eighth grade. For the first grading period, her grades were average; mostly B's and C's. Although not a strong student academically, Rene is performing at the level at which she is most comfortable and capable. Rene is usually happy, energetic, and spirited. She has had the same three friends since the first grade; they appear to enjoy one another's companionship. Up to the present, the teachers had referred to the four students as the "Fearsome Foursome." Rene, Robert, Gina, and Gabriel all performed at similar levels in the various classes: they were never at the top of the class; nor were they at the bottom. The "Fearsome Foursome" had much in common as the school year had begun. From August to October, Robert, Gina, and Gabriel had experienced significant growth and developmental spurts. The group was beginning to experience growth pains as the second grading period began.

When the students were measured for height on the first day of October, Rene was the shortest girl; she also was the shortest student in the eighth grade. The "Fearsome Foursome" became the trio with one extra. When the group met before school, in the hall, at lunch, or after school, the same subject was discussed. The discussion always began and ended the same way. Rene was shorter than any other member of the group; when the group mentioned it, she would become angry and refuse to talk to members of the group for several days.

In Miss Brown's English class, Jack sat behind her; at six feet he was very tall compared to her four feet. From the first day of the school year, Jack had teased her about her height. One Monday, Jack encouraged Byron to tease her, also. Since Rene had had a fight with her group of friends on the previous Friday, she was on her own. At first it was the usual type of irritation, but then Jack and Byron both began to hit her and whisper insults to her. After about ten minutes of the teasing, Rene began to cry. Miss Brown quickly many times in the After School Reading Program last year. She had been able to help James make progress in his reading using this program. Mrs. Poteat also had worked with his mother and had tried to encourage her with words of praise and financial support.

Since James's mother worked so much, she did not have the time to visit the school on a regular basis. She was a caring, loving mother who worked very hard to provide for her family. Her husband had left her and the family almost five years ago; during this time, she had struggled financially and physically to provide for the family. She tried to show her love and concern for the family as often as possible.

QUESTIONS

1. If you were the fourth-grade teacher, how would you handle the reading problems?
2. Would you recommend that James see a reading specialist?
3. What is James's current level of functioning?
4. How would you alter the curriculum to accommodate James?
5. How could the physical stature of James present problems?

Case Study 15
Sherry

Sherry is a fifteen-year-old girl who is in the ninth grade and academically one of the top students in her class. She was tested for and admitted to the gifted and talented classes when she was in the second grade. She is bright, pretty, witty, funny, and articulate. Sherry is the younger of two children; her parents own and operate the local drugstore. Her sister, Helen, was an average student throughout high school; she married her high school boyfriend upon graduation from high school last year.

Chad is a sixteen-year-old boy who is in the tenth grade. He lives across the street from Sherry. They have known each other since Sherry was in first grade and Chad in second. Chad and Sherry walk to school together every morning. They often work on many committees together and occasionally go to football games with other kids from school. They have been close friends and have been able to talk about almost everything. They talk easily about sex, gossip, politics, and their personal lives. They have liked each other for almost ten years. Everyone at school believes they are "going steady." They are not.

The school's annual harvest dance will be in two weeks; Sherry does not have a date. She often has gone out with a group of her friends; however, she never has had a date with only one boy. The boys she knows and talks to like her; she is popular with the boys. She usually goes to the parties with a group of friends, yet she never gets asked individually to go with one boy. Thus far, none of the boys have asked her for a date.

Sherry's mother says for her to be patient and not rush dating. Her mother says, "Sherry, you are pretty, intelligent, and popular. When the time is right, you will know it and he will know it. You just take your time. You have your whole life ahead of you. When the time is right, it will happen." Sherry and her mother have a close relationship and have been able to talk about almost everything.

Except for Sherry, all of the girls in her group of friends have had a steady boyfriend since the beginning of the school year. Up to now, Sherry has been too busy to notice that all of her girlfriends date or have a steady boyfriend. As Chad and Sherry were walking to school on Monday, she asked him what he was going to do for the harvest dance. He told her that he didn't know. He also told her that he had not thought about it and quickly changed the subject. Sherry felt that he was trying to hide something, but she didn't know what.

QUESTIONS

1. What is Sherry's current level of functioning?
2. If you were Sherry's school counselor, what suggestions would you give her about relating to Chad?
3. Is the relationship between Chad and Sherry healthy for both?
4. As Sherry's homeroom teacher, how could you alter the curriculum to provide more opportunities for helping Sherry to develop improved interpersonal skills?

Case Study 16
Jennifer

Before Jennifer entered first grade at the age of six, her parents had been divorced. The life of the family was filled with abrupt changes, constant turmoil, and long periods without adult supervision. While Jennifer was in first and second grade her life was filled with uncertainty, neglect, and physical abuse; both parent contributed to this abuse and neglect. At the beginning of the third grade, she was removed from her mother's home because of neglect and abuse. Her mother and father were using drugs on a regular basis and often left Jennifer by herself. The Division of Health and Human Services and the juvenile court severed all parental rights and placed Jennifer with her maternal grandparents.

The grandparents had agreed only reluctantly to keep Jennifer, since they were in their late sixties and both had had several heart attacks. Because of the lack of mobility of the grandmother and her related medical problems, Jennifer's aunt, May, had moved in with them to manage the household and to monitor health-related problems. Since May lived in the home and the grandparents were legally responsible for Jennifer, all three shared the responsibilities of caring for Jennifer.

Throughout the first grade, Jennifer had had difficulty with self-control and following directions. She often displayed aggressive behavior: screaming, crying, kicking, and hitting. Jennifer, her first-grade teacher, and the principal met every Friday to work on Jennifer's behavior problems. When Jennifer was corrected or directed to do something, she would scream loudly and then spend several minutes crying.

During the second grade, although severely delayed, her social skills improved. Her teacher often commented that Jennifer could not share with other children, would scream at a student who did not do what she wanted, and would argue loudly when she was disciplined for her classroom behavior. Jennifer's primary way of sharing was to grab items from others if she wanted them. In the classroom, Jennifer would take over the role of teacher, telling the other children what to do. When the students ignored her, she became aggressive.

The grandparents and aunt were cooperative and worked closely with the school to help Jennifer. At the end of the second grade, her Aunt May moved to another state. Jennifer's temper tantrums during second grade had decreased significantly, yet these behaviors were still present and occasionally appeared. Jennifer and her Aunt May had developed a good relationship; they had worked well together as a team. Everyone at the school believed that it was May who had helped Jennifer work to control her behavior at school and in the home. Now that May had left the home, it did not appear that anyone in the home was capable of managing or controlling Jennifer.

During the first week of the third grade, Jennifer demonstrated unique behavior; it was not like any that Mrs. Baker had been told to expect. Jennifer did not want to be touched physically in any form. On the playground, in the classroom, or in the hallway, she would hit, slap, kick, or yell at anyone who would touch her in any manner. She would have to be physically removed from the classroom an average of twice a week because of her tantrums. At least once during one of her tantrums, she cried and said, "I hate this school and everybody in it. You and everybody in this school hate me. I don't understand why you won't stand up for me. You let everyone in this school push me around. I don't have anyone." When she calmed down, Jennifer would always try to apologize for the behavior to Mrs. Baker, the principal, and the students in her class.

Every Friday for one month, Jennifer repeated this now predictable behavior pattern. Mrs. Baker and the principal were becoming frustrated. Everyone knew that something must be done to control Jennifer's classroom behavior.

Now at the third-grade level, Jennifer's previous temper tantrums seemed to be returning. At the beginning of the current year, Jennifer's father began to visit her at her home. The grandparents report that he would make promises that he could not or would not keep. After this happened, Jennifer would go through a period of outbursts both at home and at school. As the grandparents approach their early seventies, they find that they are not capable of managing Jennifer; they seem overwhelmed by her current behavior. It appears to them that she is returning to her previous behavior, and they do not know how to reverse it.

QUESTIONS

1. What is Jennifer's current level of functioning?
2. How can you modify the curriculum to meet Jennifer's individual and behavioral needs?

3. What would you recommend as appropriate behavioral management strategies for Jennifer in a classroom setting?
4. If you were Mrs. Baker, what specific recommendations relating to Jennifer's behavior would you make to the principal?
5. How would you, as a teacher, involve Health and Human Services or school counselors with Jennifer?

Case Study 17
Katherine

Katherine is fourteen years old and in the ninth grade. Her parents have been divorced since she was in the fourth grade; she has lived with her mother since the divorce. The mother consistently has been supportive of Katherine in all of her activities. Katherine has an older brother, Kerry, who is a senior in high school. She also has a younger sister, Kathy, who is in the seventh grade. The family is close and supportive of one another. In conversations with Katherine, she talks of helping with the household chores and other family responsibilities. This is probably because her mother works two jobs. Nothing is known of the father, as the divorce was quite bitter and he left town.

Katherine is average in height and weight for her age. She appears to be a bit awkward; however, this has not prevented her from participating in various school activities. She is a member of the cheerleader squad, is on the track team, and is active in several of the academic clubs. Katherine appears to be tired all the time, but this does not slow her down, as she pushes herself constantly. Katherine has missed school recently for minor health-related reasons. Like most teenage girls, Katherine is very concerned with her appearance. She dresses stylishly, and her hair is always neatly done. Kerry says that Katherine cannot get dressed in the morning until she has called Jean and Betsy, two of her girlfriends, to find out what they want her to wear.

Katherine is very conscious of her peer group. Her peer group contains students who are the top students in the school, and all are involved with cheerleading in some manner. The group has a reputation for stressing high standards in academics, and physical appearance; only those who meet these standards join the clique. There are high levels of competition for top grades and recognition within the group. It is generally accepted that membership in this group guarantees an individual social position in the class and in the school. When she's with her group, Katherine appears to be shy and withdrawn. Jean is the top student in the class and is the dominant personality in the group. Jean and Betsy are very conscious that they maintain their weight at exactly 110 pounds. Quite often they go without food and water for several days to maintain their weight. The girls have a weekly weight check and then decide the strategy for the week ahead.

Like everyone else in the group, Katherine likes to excel; she is able to compete with the top student for grades and honors. Socially, Katherine enjoys the company of her friends. Whether it is at school, at a party, or in the shopping mall, Katherine is seen always with Jean and Betsy. They appear to dress and talk alike. Kathy and Kerry say that every evening Katherine spends at least two hours on the phone talking with Jean and Betsy.

Katherine is a dependable person and respects those in authority. She strives to do the right thing and urges others to conform. She constantly worries about doing what she perceives as "the right thing." Around her mother, she always shows great respect. Katherine is a delightful girl who is very easygoing; she enjoys teasing her friends and teachers. Kathy says that Katherine is just "hyper because of those pills she's been taking." Katherine constantly tries to please adults, especially her male teachers.

Academically, Katherine is one of the top students and is very conscientious about her grades. Test scores demonstrate consistently that Katherine shows great potential as a student. She exhibits understanding of fundamental knowledge. Katherine likes to question alternatives. She eagerly becomes involved in discussion activities. She is punctual with her schoolwork and worries about making up work when she misses school. Kathy says that Katherine is just "obsessive."

Katherine appears to be a well-adjusted, motivated person. For the past two weeks, Katherine appears to have lost a significant amount of weight, as do Jean and Betsy. Kerry says that it is a "weight thing." Jean and Betsy maintain that Kerry is just jealous of the group's success. Kerry is an average student with average grades.

QUESTIONS

1. What is Katherine's current level of functioning? Does she have a problem?
2. Is Katherine's behavior typical of teenage behavior? Why? Give two examples of social teenage behavior.
3. Why does Katherine rely on group decisions so much?
4. How do Jean and Betsy influence her behavior?

Case Study 18
Susan

Susan is a ten-year-old girl in the third grade. She is an only child who lives with her mother and grandfather. Susan has never seen her father; her mother refuses all attempts to talk about him. The grandfather is in his early seventies; he does not hide the fact that he resents Susan and her mother living with him. According to the neighbors, it is a daily argument the family has. As a sales representative, Susan's mother is away from home a great deal of the time; she does, however, try to spend quality time with Susan. Because of her travel schedule, Susan's mother rarely visits the school; the grandfather has represented the mother during all of the staffing, Individual Educational Plan (IEP), and teacher conferences.

In the second grade, Susan had been identified as having specific learning disabilities in math; she receives daily support from an itinerant learning disabilities (LD) teacher. Specific behavioral objectives were included in the initial IEP but later were removed after a hearing to resolve objections raised by the mother's legal counsel. Susan has taken the medication Ritalin with one dose administered at school since she entered the first grade. From the first grade, her behavior has stood in the way of her learning. She repeated kindergarten and the first grade; both teachers had expressed concerns about her bizarre behavior. Susan's reputation in the school was established in kindergarten by her screaming, yelling, rolling on the floor, and running the halls after being chosen last for jump rope; these behaviors were predictable following any stressful situation that Susan encountered.

Mrs. Kelly, her third grade teacher, stated that daily Susan used many childish and immature behaviors to get her own way. She often used tears or the act of crying to gain attention for her being injured, real or often imagined. Mrs. Kelly stated that the most common statement is "Julie, or Jane, or Mike is making fun of me, make her/him stop." She cried this week because another child told her where to write her name on the chalkboard. She also cried because someone said she had never been to a neighboring small town. She also cried because her reading team was going too fast and she couldn't keep up with them. On Monday when Mrs. Kelly was absent, Susan sobbed all day; she continually asked for her mother or for Mrs. Kelly.

Friday afternoon recess was the major tantrum of the school year. One student's parent had brought a German shepherd to show the class. All of the students in the class were given an opportunity to pet and hug the dog. After all the children had a turn petting the dog, Susan rushed back up to the dog and hugged it tightly. When the parent pulled the dog away and began to leave, she began screaming and rolling on the floor. The parent, visibly shaken by the scene, had to be assisted from the school building.

The class has become anesthetized to Susan's range of behaviors. She often sits with all four fingers in her mouth, or constantly hums, or inappropriately sings out loud, or sits in the corner of the room under her coat. She engages in more serious behaviors, such as biting herself and others, hitting, and kicking. She slaps anyone who cuts in line or makes remarks to her. The class, as a whole, has a high level of tolerance for her assorted behaviors; often they tease and encourage her in many of these behaviors. Usually, the teasing is a result of many days of Susan being the center of attention in the class. It is apparent that as the members of the class develop and mature, the differences between them and Susan widen.

Susan does not know how to study, work quietly, or begin an assignment. The top of the desk becomes piled high with things as she decides what to do first. For her to complete an assignment requires that Mrs. Kelly spend the morning sitting beside Susan dictating every step and motion. When Mrs. Kelly would leave her to help another student, Susan would either go into a tantrum or she would follow Mrs. Kelly.

Mrs. Kelly sent a note to the principal that appeared to summarize Susan and her unique situation. She wrote, "The increased demands of the third-grade curriculum are too much for Susan. She doesn't work well independently, and she doesn't work well with a team. She will only produce on a one-to-one basis with me or with the special education teacher. In one more year this child will be in a middle school environment, changing classes hourly and being responsible for herself. How will she cope? How can I possibly get this child ready for the middle school in the four months that remain of school? I don't know what to do!"

QUESTIONS

1. What is Susan's current level of functioning?
2. Specifically, what would you do to improve Susan's self-concept?

3. What modification in the curriculum would you make to involve Susan more in the classroom activities?
4. How can Susan be taught organizational skills, self-motivation, and responsibility?

Case Study 19
Jan and Dan

Jan and Dan are identical twin boys who are thirteen years old and in the seventh grade. They have been active in all of the athletic programs at the school; they always have received recognition for their successes in basketball, baseball, football, and track and field. The boys have been equally successful in the classroom; they have made the honor roll consistently since the fourth grade. They have received recognition from their coaches and teachers for the dedication and reliability that they bring to any endeavor.

Two weeks before the beginning of the school term this year, the boys' parents divorced. The boys now live with the mother and an aunt, Kate; the father lives in another part of the state. The divorce was not a pleasant affair for anyone; everyone left the courtroom changed. The father was to have visitation rights every two weeks, but after two months, he refused to see the boys or communicate with them in any manner. He had blamed the mother for the breakup of the family and many of the problems of the marriage. The boys were thoroughly confused; they did not know which side was being honest with them.

Living in Aunt Kate's house also was a difficult change for the boys; they now share a room, whereas before each boy had his own room. More often now Kate would refer to them as "you two" rather than Jan and Dan. The boys were being forced into situations that pushed them together as a "pair."

Examining the boys on a casual basis, it is hardly possible to believe they are identical. The boys have many interests and developments that are different. Jan has a steady girlfriend; Dan does not. Dan likes to draw and paint; Jan does not. Jan likes to write poetry; Dan likes to write short stories. Jan likes drama; Dan likes debating.

During the past two weeks, the relationship with the mother has begun to resemble that of the relationship with the father. The most dominant adult figure in the boys' lives is Kate. Aunt Kate and her husband have become the foster parents for the boys. They attend all of the boys' school, athletic, and social events.

QUESTIONS

1. What is the current level of functioning for Jan and Dan?
2. What can be done within a classroom setting that will encourage the development of each boy individually?
3. As the school counselor, how can you help the boys adjust to the changes within their lives?
4. As a teacher, how can you alter the curriculum to help Jan and Dan?

UNIT 3
Moral Development

Case Study 20
Three Students

Graham was the oldest of three children and an eighteen-year-old senior in a new high school. Prior to this year, Graham had attended the local private high school; at the end of the school year, he had been asked to leave because of grades, behavior, and attendance. While at the private high school, he had had numerous disciplinary problems, ranging from talking back to his teachers to abusive behavior toward other students. When he talked with the guidance counselor there, Graham said he had never wanted to go to the private high school. The guidance counselor told Graham that to remain at the private school he had to maintain at least a C average.

Marcia is fifteen years old. She and Graham had been dismissed from the private high school for almost the same reasons. Before being dismissed from the private high school, Marcia had maintained an F in all of her classes. Marcia's teachers had said that she had the ability to achieve superior grades if she applied herself and learned how to study. Now in the public school her grades ranged from a C to an F, and Marcia, like Graham, had many confrontations with the principal, the assistant principal, and the dean of the students. She maintained that none of the school's administration understood what it was like to be young. She was in the in-school suspension class every other day for most of the year. Marcia would constantly sass, talk back to, or mock her teachers as the mood struck her. She never took her class assignments seriously; during class time, she would try to talk with all the girls who sat around her. On Mondays, she would describe in great detail what she and her friends had done over the weekend; most of the actions centered on her drinking, driving, and being sexually active.

This was Marty's first year at the junior high school. He was anxious about attending public school, although he had attended the public elementary school. Before the end of the school year, Marty and Graham had broken into the private school and had destroyed two of the restrooms. The court had placed the boys on probation, and ordered that they pay for the damages and do sixty hours of community work. When Marty was asked to leave at the end of the school year, it was hard for him to accept. For the past five years, he had attended the prestigious private elementary school. For four years, he had been on the honor rolls and received many awards for his academic work. Academic work was easy for Marty; he never had to work very hard to achieve good grades or recognition. In the athletics or the physical education classes, Marty was an average student. He always enjoyed sports, games, or contests, yet he recognized that he was not very good at them. He always had admired Graham; they had been close pals.

These three children and their parents had always lived in the industrial town. The father was a vice president of one of the local factories, and the mother taught psychology at the local community college. Both parents were embarrassed by their children's actions. After the court trial of Graham and Marty, they had all three children visit a child psychiatrist on a weekly basis. After a while the children convinced their parents that they had learned their lessons and would change their behavior.

School has been in session for almost six weeks; grade cards will be issued at the end of the week. Unfortunately for the family, nothing has changed. The children's grades and behavior and the actions of the parents are the same as before; the only change has been the location of the children.

QUESTIONS

1. As Marty's advisor, what specific things can you do to help him?
2. As Marcia's English teacher, what specific actions would you take?
3. As the school counselor, what would you advise Graham to do?
4. How would you involve the parents in discussions with the children?
5. As Graham's U.S. history teacher, what specific actions would you take?

Case Study 21
Marcus—Young and Gifted

Marcus is two years old and the youngest of three children. He has an older brother, Derek, who is eleven, and a sister, Judy, who is thirteen. Marcus is shorter than average and began walking at about eight months of age. Marcus never experienced the crawling stage; he simply skipped it and began to walk from the beginning. From the moment he began to walk at eight months, he quickly became the center of attention. He was so small that people assumed that he was much younger than he actually was.

Marcus gave all of the appearances of a typical two-year-old; however, these were manifested when he was only nine months old. Since he was able to walk, he was investigating everything; he could be seen pulling the contents out of cabinets and knocking items off shelves. Marcus gave new meaning to the term "the Terrible Twos." It was said that he could and did demolish everything at eye level or hand level. Nothing was safe if it was in his line of vision.

Time has passed with many battles having been waged between Marcus and everyone around him. He continues to be an extremely active child; he is unable to sit still or keep quiet for even a very short period of time—ten seconds is the maximum. His physical activity continues from the moment he awakens in the morning until he passes out from exhaustion at night. When Marcus goes to sleep, it is as if he has gone into hibernation. He falls into a deep sleep that lasts for almost six and a half hours.

Both of his parents resist any attempt at taking Marcus to any social event. Sunday services are not a thing that the family looks forward to enduring. When his father, brother, sister, or mother holds him during the worship services, a wrestling match or major battle is contested. Typically, he can be observed stretching, reaching, falling backwards, climbing up the front of a person, or grabbing and holding onto the parishioner's head. Marcus will grab, pinch, swing at, or swat at anyone next to him, in front of him, or behind him. If he connects with one of his blows, he will laugh hysterically.

It appears that Marcus considers everything within reach as a lethal weapon. If he can manage to hold it, it will be thrown. However, when given cards with pictures on them, he will look intently at them and talk while holding them. A major scene erupts if anyone attempts to take the cards from him. Once during a Sunday evening service, his sister tried to take the cards from him to get him to stop talking so loudly. He yelled, kicked, screamed, and hit her so much that the services stopped. Everyone in the church turned to look at him. When Judy gave in to him and left him alone, he threw the cards up into the air and laughed loudly.

Marcus constantly speaks in words, phrases, and some sentences. He has always spoken in distinct, clear words and phrases; there was never a period of time that he repeated words spoken to him. Last week in church, he repeated his sister's name in sing-song fashion for about five minutes. When the service became quiet, he stated over and over, "I'm gonna cut you up, I'm gonna stab you, then I'll just eat you up." His father had to take him outside to prevent a near riot in the church.

One of his preferred games is a kind of hide-and-seek and tag up and down the aisles of the church. His attention span is so short that nothing his family provides occupies him for long. These antics do not make him or his family very popular with the members of the Sunday worship services.

Academically, Marcus has demonstrated consistently superior skills. Although he is two years old, he reads almost at the ninth-grade level. His math skills have been evaluated to be at the ninth- or tenth-grade level. His parents have tried to find educational settings that would be challenging and intellectually stimulating. Since he is almost three years old, Marcus has been placed in each of the following: Head Start, pre-kindergarten classes, MENSA study classes, kindergarten classes, many behavioral disorder classes, workshop centers, and private baby-sitting. The longest time he was able to stay at any of these was the three days he stayed with a baby-sitter. The baby-sitter had been keeping one other child who was five years old, and Marcus and this child fought constantly for two days. The baby-sitter finally told the parents to never bring Marcus back to her.

QUESTIONS

1. If you had Marcus in a classroom setting, how would you deal with his short attention span?
2. How is Marcus a "normal" two-year-old child?
3. What short-term suggestions do you have for the parents?
4. What long-term suggestions do you have for the family?
5. If Marcus were to be recommended for screening and assessment, what specific suggestions would you provide to the behavioral specialist?

Case Study 22
Jefferson

Jefferson is eleven years old, but physically he looks to be about fourteen or fifteen. He has never failed any grade and has never started school late. He is interesting, funny and bright. He qualified for the gifted program at school when he was in the second grade. He wants to be a biochemical engineer like his father, and he already has chosen a college and has received information about their programs.

Jefferson is in Mrs. Hine's fifth grade, and she finds him to be one of the best, brightest, and most well-balanced students she has taught in her twenty years of teaching. She praises, defends, and counsels with Jefferson constantly. They make a rather "odd couple." From the moment Jefferson arrives in the morning until the end of the day, except when he's in art or gym class, Jefferson sits close to Mrs. Hine. They talk about many things inside the classroom, at lunch, during recess, and before and after school.

The major interests in Jefferson's life are computers, high school and college sports, and high school life in general. His brother, Jesse, who is seventeen, is a junior at the local high school. Jesse spends as little time with Jefferson as possible. Jesse is an average student who maintains a C average in most of his subjects in school. Many of the friends and neighbors say that Jefferson and Jesse fight constantly when they are both at home. The fights are about the same issue: Jesse doing what Jefferson wants to do. When pressed, the parents admit that the boys occasionally do have trouble relating to each other. They generally dismiss questions about the boys' problems as being something that boys naturally do, and they maintain that the boys are just good, friendly, high-spirited rivals.

Jefferson is a natural leader. At recess, no matter who brings out the ball, everyone waits for Jefferson to organize the game, determine who plays where, and create the rules of the day. During the past three years, his classes have never deviated from this routine when Jefferson is present. No one has ever argued with him as to where, why, and what game is to be played or the organization for the game. It is truly amazing to see.

Jefferson has a sharp wit, which often gets him into trouble with adults and several older students. His mother is quiet and soft-spoken, and she has always used reason in dealing with Jefferson. She maintains that he is a sensitive boy who needs to have things explained to him. Anytime that Jefferson has done something wrong or she has been unhappy with his behavior, she has sat down with him and explained exactly what he did and the rationale for making amends for it. The father has never had to deal with the discipline of the boys; the mother has been the primary disciplinarian. Jefferson's father seems to be almost invisible. When the family has been seen at the school, his father has always been in the background, never commenting or speaking to the boys.

Jefferson likes to argue, debate, and do lots of verbal sparring with anyone who will participate. He finds this entertaining and never seems to tire of the game. However, when any teacher or adult would refuse to play the game with him, he would become angry. In the past, it has appeared that his anger would become consuming and driving; he would begin using loud, abusive, and obscene language and gestures. When violence appeared evident, he would retreat to a safe distance and try to continue his verbal abuse.

Last year, a week before the holidays were to begin, he had a terrible argument with the art teacher. Mr. Griffin had collected all of the art supplies before the class was to leave. Jefferson had taken a piece of yarn and tied it around his neck. Mr. Griffin asked Jefferson for the yarn. When he refused, Mr. Griffin removed the yarn from Jefferson's neck. Jefferson grabbed the yarn, wrapped it several times around his neck, and tied it into a hard knot. Within minutes, he began to turn blue. Mr. Griffin sent the class out of the room, called for help from Mr. Wells across the hall, and proceeded to remove the yarn from Jefferson's neck. When the yarn was removed, Jefferson stated loudly, "That ought to teach you to mess with me, smarty!" Jefferson was suspended from school for three days. Mr. Griffin and Jefferson wage combat from the beginning of the class to the end of it. Jefferson enjoys art but does not have the patience or talent for the class.

In Mr. Howard's physical education class, Jefferson is a terror. When he is not sitting on the bleachers for talking rudely to other students or Mr. Howard, he is sitting in the assistant principal's office for having said one too many obscene words to Mr. Howard. Jefferson is not physically talented enough to do all that is required in physical education class.

Jefferson's mother explains his difficulty in art and physical education as examples of his acting out his frustrations. He expects perfection of himself even though he doesn't have the physical abilities to do them. It is frustrating for him to see others do things easily when he has such great difficulty performing. Because he demands perfection of himself, he is not a good sport about losing, failing, or being reminded that he cannot do something. The staff, teachers, and students generally view Jefferson as hostile to those whom he dislikes. They believe he makes insulting and rude remarks to everyone.

QUESTIONS

1. As Jefferson's art teacher, what specific changes would you make in the curriculum to involve him more?
2. Can you explain to Mr. Howard why Jefferson behaves the way he does?
3. What changes to Jefferson's curriculum would you make?
4. How could you involve Jesse with helping Jefferson to develop interpersonal skills?

Case Study 23
Patricia

Patricia is an eighteen-year-old high school senior. Her parents are well-to-do, and their children always have had the most stylish clothes, the most expensive shoes, and every current fad. Of four siblings, she is the oldest girl and the second oldest child in a family that encourages and practices competition in all aspects of the family life.

Although not considered a very pretty girl, Patricia has a pleasant smile and a very personable personality that seems to attract people. Patricia always has been the one picked for the front row, the lead in the play, the one to sing the solo, and the one to represent the student body. This type of favoritism has followed Patricia from the first grade through the twelfth grade; many students, parents, and teachers have resented strongly her selection for events. Patricia has had the ability to relate to a wide variety of individuals; at social gatherings, people instantly are attracted to her.

Patricia is intellectually superior to almost all of the students, staff, and faculty in the high school. When she was in the seventh grade, the local college asked her parents to permit Patricia to register for several of the courses during the evening. She had little trouble passing the courses with a 4.0 average. The college requested that she be admitted to the degree program on a full-time basis; her parents refused, and Patricia returned to the regular junior high school curriculum. She had made the transition from junior high school to college and back to junior high school with few adjustments. After the seventh grade, Patricia never mentioned college again.

At the beginning of the school year, Patricia discovered boys. Previously, none of the boys considered her more than "one of the guys"; then she discovered Patrick. Patrick was everything that Patricia was not. He was handsome, obsessive, manipulative, cruel, dishonest, and unreliable. To Patricia, Patrick was wise, kind, thoughtful, and dependable; he became her boyfriend. Patrick became the center of her life. He would compliment and praise her one minute and then criticize and ignore her the next. Everyone at the high school can pinpoint the exact day that Patricia began to show signs of having multiple personalities.

When Patricia and Patrick began to go steady, Patricia began showing severe periods of moodiness and depressions. She would ignore former friends then and just as suddenly begin to talk to them again thus creating rivalries among the friends. Patricia would use minor mistakes as cause for creating major confrontations with various students. She was hot and cold with friends. They weren't sure from day to day how she would treat them. From September to January, Patricia's friends slowly began to avoid her. By the end of February, Patricia had one friend, Patrick. This led to Patricia's being placed in the hospital for two weeks; she received treatment for severe depression.

On Monday, Patricia is to return to the high school. Patrick has found a new girlfriend; therefore, he did not visit Patricia at the hospital.

QUESTIONS

1. What is Patricia's current level of functioning?
2. If you were Patricia's homeroom teacher, what would you do when she arrived in your class?
3. If you were a school counselor, what would you do when Patricia returned on Monday?
4. How could you help Patricia manage the loss of a boyfriend?

Children with Special Problems

Case Study 24
Chris

Chris is a nine-year-old boy in the third grade; he is the youngest student in the class. In birth order, he is next to the youngest in a family of eight children. His younger sister, Cathy, who is six, is in the kindergarten class. There are ten years' difference between Chris and his older brother, Charles. Both his mother and father work; therefore, the oldest sister, Becky, who is thirty-two years old, had assumed the primary responsibility for caring for the family. Since his birth, Becky has treated Chris as her own son; she carefully watches him to ensure that he doesn't get hurt or get into any trouble. It was due to Becky's influence that Chris was enrolled in the first grade at age five.

Chris had a most difficult time adjusting to the first grade. The teacher and the principal had tried to convince Becky and his parents to enroll Chris one year later; they strongly refused. All throughout the first grade, Chris had difficulty concentrating, paying attention, staying on task, and working independently. During the second grade, the problems continued. The second-grade teacher recommended that Chris be retained in the first grade rather than be admitted to the second grade because of his immature behavior. Becky and the parents objected to the recommendation, and Chris was placed in the second grade. Academically, Chris ranks between average and above average. He grasps concepts quickly when he sits and concentrates on the idea. He has consistently scored above grade level on all of the standardized tests that he has taken.

The beginning of the school year was similar to what it had been in the other grades; Chris was out of control. As the morning began, Chris would sit for a moment and listen to his teacher, Mrs. Hanson, giving instructions. Before she had finished, Chris would be walking around the class, looking out of the window, or playing with the fish in the aquarium. According to Mrs. Hanson, who is his third-grade teacher, Chris has a serious behavior problem; he has had a very short attention span in class. He often can be observed staring out into space when he should be working. Frequently during the class, he will sing, hum, or make faces at the other students.

His teachers have described his behavior as childish, silly, and distracting. The other students in the class have a very difficult time trying to understand why Chris does what he does. Chris has had many other problems relating to the members of the class. Several times during the day, Chris will take things from the desks, play with them, and then throw the item out of the window or into the trash.

From the first week of school, Chris has developed and maintained poor relationships with the members of his class. The students seem to resent Chris for his silly antics, disturbing the class and irritating students as they work on the class assignments. As the first week of school ended, the students began to take out their aggression on Chris verbally and physically. At every opportunity, they tease and taunt him. When the teacher is not around, they harass and physically attack Chris. During recess or in the gym, Chris often ends the period playing by himself. If one were to ask individual members of the class, they would name Chris as the least popular student in the class.

QUESTIONS

1. What is Chris's current level of functioning? Strengths? Weaknesses?
2. How can Mrs. Hanson help Chris to develop control over his behavior?
3. How can the curriculum be altered to provide opportunities for Chris to learn more effectively?
4. How can Chris learn from cooperative learning experiences?

Case Study 25
Joseph

Joseph is seven years old and is the middle child in his family. His older sister is ten and his younger brother five. His mother stays home to care for the family; she takes special interest in the progress that Joe is making in school. Both of the parents are concerned about Joseph's academic progress and personal behavior in school. The family is generally present during PTA meetings, school events, and social events that involve their children. Both parents are extremely busy in their private and family lives, yet they try to make time for school events.

In Mrs. Wayne's second-grade classroom, Joseph sits in the front of the class. He has worn special glasses since kindergarten, yet he still has great difficulty seeing the chalkboard. Mrs. Wayne always provides him with a copy of all written instructions and classwork written on the board. She writes the instructions, extra large so that Joseph can see them clearly. There are twenty-five students in the second-grade class; the extra work requires that Mrs. Wayne plan carefully what she will talk about each day. Joseph is a good reader and excels at games involving words. He often says that his favorite subjects are spelling and language arts.

Joseph does not like mathematics in any form; he will sulk, delay, and wait until the last possible moment to turn in his math assignments. His grades in math consistently have been D's. It is rare that Joseph would receive a grade higher than sixty-five in his math class. As to science, he enjoys the class and does quite well.

Since the beginning of school, Joseph has had many problems with his vision. It is now approaching Halloween, and his vision is becoming worse. Despite using his glasses and a large magnifying glass, Joseph still has problems reading the print in books, worksheets, and instruction sheets. No matter how large Mrs. Wayne writes on the board, Joseph has problems recognizing letters, numbers, and words. The parents have told Mrs. Wayne that the optometrist says that he cannot prescribe any glasses that will improve Joseph's vision.

Joseph is popular with the other members of the class. When they notice that Joseph is having problems with reading, they quickly move closer to him and read the words to him. At first, Joseph enjoyed the attention from his classmates, but that was almost two months ago. Today, the attention that he has been receiving is frustrating to him. He wants to see better, yet he knows that his vision is not improving.

During the reading class on Wednesday morning, Joseph and his vision problem reached a climax. He and several students had a disagreement over who would help him read. Following a terrible yelling, pushing, and slapping incident, Mrs. Wayne called his parents; she made a Monday afternoon appointment to meet with them, Joseph, the principal, and the special education teacher.

QUESTIONS

1. How should the teacher prepare for the conference with Joseph's parents?
2. What specific things would you recommend in dealing with Joseph within a classroom setting?
3. What observations should the teacher bring to the meeting?
4. How can the curriculum be altered to meet Joseph's needs?

Case Study 26
Donnie

Donnie is sixteen years old; he is in Mrs. Well's junior high school resource room. He has been at the junior high school for five years. Donnie is physically larger and more developed than all the other students in the eighth grade. Many of the students consider him to be likable and friendly, and he tries to please all of his teachers. He is aware of his limitations, yet he works hard in all of his classes.

Donnie was tested and qualified for special education when he was in the second grade. At that time, he qualified for services for educable mentally handicapped students. He has worked well in many of the one-to-one encounters and responds to individual attention, praise, and encouragement from adults. When faced with difficult tasks and decisions, Donnie becomes frustrated, stubborn, and resistive. His behavior becomes loud and disruptive when he meets challenges that he fears he cannot conquer. He gives up easily at times and refuses to continue on tasks that make him feel incompetent and slow.

On days when everything is going well, Donnie shows maturity in behavior, judgment, and a strong desire to succeed both academically and socially. During this time, he works consistently and speaks well of himself and others. His interactions with both peers and adults are positive yet quite limited.

Socially, Donnie's skills are depressed and crude. He has chosen to interact with a peer group composed generally of twelve- and thirteen-year-old students. Although members of the group and Donnie share few interests, he seems to feel secure with this age group. Membership in this group also presents many difficult problems for him. He is often isolated, lonely, and unaccepted within this peer group; quite often he looks to adults for acceptance and recognition. Donnie recently has become sexually active; this is a major concern for his parents and teachers. Donnie has not chosen partners well; he has chosen partners who are eleven and twelve years old.

Donnie's attitude toward other students closer to his age and the resulting problems arise from his hostile and aggressive behavior toward them. However, not all of the problems are created by Donnie. Many of the students of his age tease and taunt him; they see him as an easy target because of his below-average mental ability. It is quite apparent that Donnie is physically different from other students at the junior high school. He lacks the social skills necessary to deal with the negative pressure he receives from peers, which often results in verbal confrontation.

Donnie appears to need constant reassurance that his contributions are valued by those around him. He sometimes seems torn between what he wants to do and what he knows is acceptable to do. Through his mistakes, he has learned that some activities are forbidden and that guilt occurs after committing these actions. None of these lessons have been easy for him or his parents to accept.

He can see the relationship between completing a task and the rewards that go with it. His difficulty with coping with academics, group activities, and peers has led to a growing sense of inferiority. The differences between him and the students at the junior high school are increasing with time. Each month and year Donnie recognizes that he has few friends and few things in common with other students. He has been frustrated and angry for most of the first grading period.

QUESTIONS

1. What is Donnie's current level of functioning?
2. How can the curriculum be altered to meet Donnie's individual needs?
3. If you were one of Donnie's teachers, how could you help him to improve his social skills?
4. When would you recommend that Donnie begin to explore a sheltered workshop setting?

Case Study 27
Jason

The students in Jason's ninth-grade classes describe him as a tall, skinny, and handicapped boy with a bad case of acne. Jason is in Mr. White's United States history class. During the first semester, he struggled in the class to make a D. During a conference with Mr. White, Jason agreed that he had not studied much. Jason promised that he would go to the study sessions and apply himself to the class.

Jason has two difficulties. One is that he is fifteen years old; as a teenager, he wants to belong to his peer group and does not want to be identified as being different. The other problem is that he has a handicap; when he is under stress, Jason stutters a great deal. Also, Jason was born with one arm half the size and length of the other arm. He has been able to use the deformed arm on a limited basis.

As an only child, Jason has had to find ways of amusing himself. Both parents work long hours in their business; therefore, he has had to spend a lot of time alone. Jason has had many difficulties with the development of interpersonal and social skills. He's never held any job outside the home; the only job that he has at home is to cut the grass. Everything that he has wanted from his parents he has received. Having money and possessions has not helped Jason socially with his peers. Many of his peers consider him odd and not able to join their groups.

Jason has had academic problems from the first day of high school. He has maintained a low C average throughout his years in school. He admits that he does not know how to study, take notes, or write class papers, yet he does not do anything about these problems. All of his teachers at the high school have offered him additional help with his studies; he has not accepted any of their offers. The school counselor meets with him every Thursday afternoon; thus far, Jason has made no progress in his classes. His teachers describe him as a "loner" and quite difficult to reach. One teacher commented, "He seems to be in his own little world that lets no one inside. He is a strange child. I find that I have a great deal of trouble talking to and getting information from him. He seems to tune me out."

QUESTIONS

1. What is Jason's current level of functioning?
2. As the teacher in a classroom setting, what specific things could you do to give Jason opportunities to improve his self-image and self-confidence?
3. What cooperative learning exercises would provide learning experiences for Jason?
4. In addition to speech therapy, what activities would you recommend for use with Jason to develop confidence with his speech?
5. As the classroom teacher, what could you do or say to Jason and / or the class that would lessen the stress of emphasizing Jason's deformed arm?

Children from Broken Homes

Case Study 28
Glenn and Bobby

Glenn lives with his father, a new stepmother, and her three children, who are ages six, seven, and eight. He shares a bedroom with his stepbrother, Bobby, who is six years old. Glenn is fifteen years old and is finishing his freshman year in high school. His father got married two weeks before the beginning of school; however, the family did not move into the new home until a week after school had started.

Glenn and his father had lived together for almost two years; his parents had divorced after many unhappy years together. As his parent's only child, Glenn had had his own room, and he had been used often as their go-between for almost three years. Glenn developed many social and communication skills during this period; he also developed maturity that was apparent to all in the junior high school.

Glenn has always had to work hard for the grades he achieves. He has received encouragement from his teachers for the progress he's made in his studies. Glenn's grades have been A's and B's; often during the three years in junior high school, he has made the honor roll. High school will be a challenge for him; he will have to learn to study and apply his energies with greater consistency. The high school is much larger than the junior high school, and he will have to ride a bus about four miles from his home to the high school.

Bobby is a young boy desperately seeking acceptance and approval, typical behavior for his age group. Up to this week, he always had slept with his mother; now he is sleeping in a bed alone and is sleeping in a room with a person he hardly knows. This is a frightening time for Bobby; he believes that everything has changed.

He talks almost nonstop to his new brother and roommate. Bobby wants Glenn to do lots of things with him. He wants Glenn to listen to him read, play ball with him, and sit next to him at dinner. During this first week, Bobby has had numerous problems adjusting to school. His two sisters made the transition to the new school with few problems; they had each other to walk, play, and talk with. Bobby wants the teacher and the students in his class to listen to him tell his stories.

Many of the problems that Bobby finds himself getting into result from his attention-getting behaviors. Bobby is the type of student that almost requires total isolation from the rest of the class. The teacher must move Bobby to various parts in the classroom three or four times during the course of the year to find out where he can best function. Bobby requires direct instruction and continual attention; otherwise, he has a difficult time staying on task and finishing any assignment. Bobby is hyperactive, is academically limited, and has a difficult time adjusting to the school environment.

QUESTIONS

1. What is Bobby's current level of functioning? What is Glenn's current level of functioning? Strengths? Weaknesses?
2. If you were Bobby's classroom teacher, how could you alter the curriculum to provide opportunities for Bobby to develop his self-image and self-concept?
3. If you were the high school guidance counselor, how could you help Glenn adjust to his new school, friends, and family?
4. This family is in transition. As a classroom teacher, should you become involved in the social dynamics of this family?

Case Study 29
Mitchell

It was the last day of Millard High School's third grading period; Mitchell Amos had lived with his grandmother and mother almost the entire school year. His parents were divorced at the beginning of this school year, and in accordance with the divorce settlement, the boys had been separated and assigned one to each of the parents. Mitchell was to live with their mother, and his brother, Morris, with their father. At first, Mitchell had seen his father every two weeks without fail, but during the past two months, his father visited him only once. Also, for a variety of reasons and family circumstances, Mitchell and his brother had developed a mutual distrust and dislike for each other. Since both boys were at Millard High School, Mitchell consciously tried to avoid his brother. When they did meet at school or after school, they greeted each other coolly, and their interaction was strained.

His father, Clyde Amos, had developed a great dislike for his ex-wife and her mother; therefore, he did not like to visit Mitchell at the grandmother's house. However, with no other place for the family to visit, Clyde Amos and the two boys had to meet at the grandmother's house. Every visit ended the same way, with lots of yelling and fierce arguing between mother and father. After the father's visits, feelings of tremendous stress and anxiety would be expressed by everyone.

At fifteen years old, Mitchell was handsome and very well developed physically; he looked to be twenty years old. He was much taller, heavier, and physically more advanced than any other member of the freshman class. Mitchell's physical abilities and talents had resulted in his being the first freshman at Millard High School to be promoted to the first string of the varsity football team; he was the first athlete from Millard High School to earn all-conference and all-state honors as a freshman. It was an event that had been carried by all of the local media for most of the football season. Following the football season, Mitchell became a school and community celebrity throughout the remainder of his freshman year. His mother and grandmother made him feel special; however, his father and brother never mentioned the publicity or acknowledged that anything special had occurred.

From the first day in Miss Davis's art class, Mitchell had become special to her. He demonstrated a tremendous, natural gift for painting and sculpture. At the end of each class period, he would thank Miss Davis for introducing him to art. As the year progressed, Mitchell's talent in art and his relationship with Miss Davis seemed to have blossomed. During the school's fall art festival, he had received an honorable mention for his watercolor painting. During the county's spring art festival, Mitchell had won a second place ribbon for his sculpture. Miss Davis had taught art at the school for fifteen years, and Mitchell was the most talented student she had ever had in her classes. She made an effort to encourage Mitchell to pursue his talents in art.

During all of Mitchell's freshman year, he had people around him. Boys and girls seemed to enjoy his personality and would follow him from place to place. In the library, in the cafeteria, or in study hall, Mitchell always had people around him. Mitchell never had a girlfriend; there were girls he liked to talk to but never a special girlfriend.

Mrs. Grey, his English teacher, was his favorite teacher. He sat near her in the lunchroom, in the library, or in school assemblies and he asked her opinion about everything that happened to him during the day. Mrs. Grey never criticized him or talked unkindly to him; she spent the time that Mitchell needed in explaining any problem. Mrs. Grey had always treated him like one of her own three children. One of Mrs. Grey's children, Matt, was Mitchell's age. Mitchell enjoyed visiting Mrs. Grey's home and having meals with them. Mitchell especially liked the special attention that Matt always would give him. Before the end of the school year, Matt and Mitchell were best friends; they tried to do many things together. Mitchell tried to spend as much of his time at Matt's house as he was allowed. The summer had been much like the rest of the school year; Matt and Mitchell were seen everywhere together.

The beginning of his sophomore year began like the freshman year had ended. Mitchell was the center of attention from the local and state media. At the beginning of October, Matt started going steady with Rachel, a girl who lived across the street from his house. For the first two weeks, Matt, Rachel, and Mitchell would try to go out together; this always would end awkwardly for Mitchell. No matter what Matt and Rachel did, Mitchell told them that he felt that he was interfering with their date.

On a Friday afternoon after a morning together, Mitchell told Matt and Rachel about his feelings of interfering with their dates. Matt and Rachel tried to reassure Mitchell; however, the more that they tried to reassure him, the more irritated he became. After this exchange, Mitchell and Matt did not see each other again. Mitchell did not go to Mrs. Grey's house or stop by to see her at school. He refused to talk to Matt, Mr. Grey, or Mrs. Grey on the telephone.

Mitchell's football coach, Miss Davis, his mother, and a majority of the school can identify the day that Mitchell's life changed. Today Mitchell no longer plays football or paints; he quietly sits in each of his classes. Thanksgiving holidays are approaching and Mitchell has maintained his isolation from everyone and everything at school. He has refused to talk to the school counselor, the principal, or his school advisor. When he was summoned to the principal's office to talk about his problems, he sat quietly, listened to the principal, and at the end of the session left without having said anything.

QUESTIONS

1. What is the problem?
2. How can Mrs. Grey help Mitchell? Should she? Why?
3. If you were Mitchell's mother, what would you do to help Mitchell?
4. If you were Miss Davis, what would you do?

Case Study 30
Chuck

Returning from the midyear holiday break, Chuck, who is in the third grade, celebrated his birthday; he is nine years old. Chuck's mother had remarried last year after a very bitter and long divorce trial. Following the divorce, Chuck's father disappeared, and in the past year and a half, no one has heard from him. Since the divorce, Chuck has been afraid of males, especially male teachers. His stepfather does not have a forceful personality, and generally relies on Chuck's mother for any decisions affecting the family. The mother has demonstrated a controlling and forceful personality. Since the marriage, his mother has devoted the majority of her time caring for Jake, Chuck's two-year-old stepbrother.

Chuck has been in the gifted program of the school since the second grade. To say that he is intelligent is an understatement. On three different standardized tests, Chuck achieved an IQ of 171. He is in the 99th percentile in reading, is in the 98th percentile in math, and has a composite score in the 98th percentile. Chuck consistently has demonstrated his unique talents and creative abilities during the past year. He developed his own robot for the science fair, wrote a play for the students, and played the clarinet for the school assembly program. He has refused all attempts to show him special attention, usually replying, "Everyone can do what I did. It's nothing really special."

Mrs. Green has twenty-two students in the third grade; Chuck seems to occupy almost half of her time and attention. Mrs. Green tries to listen attentively to Chuck as he explains causes for the variety of problems he faces each day. The problems range from not being appropriately or adequately dressed for school to arguments with the school bus driver over driving the bus too fast.

Organization is not Chuck's strongest asset. When asked to turn in his homework, he usually has a puzzled look on his face as he reaches into his book bag. He always carries a large suitcase containing all of his books, music, and papers. This is not your typical book bag. It is a very large carpet-bag with all kinds of crumpled papers inside. After about five minutes, Chuck produces a wrinkled piece of paper. He is aware of the sloppy appearance, yet he is unprepared to alter this image.

Chuck has few friends, and they tend to be younger than he is. Except for his intellect, Chuck is incapable of acting like a child of his age. He has problems socially working with other people his own age. He has become a loner in most of the classroom activities.

Chuck has a sense of humor that appeals to adults more so than to young people. He has a quick mind that keeps his teachers alert. He has great vocabulary and language skills, but doesn't write well. He is a terrible speller, and his work is sloppy. Despite all of these shortcomings, Chuck is a very interesting individual.

QUESTIONS

1. What is Chuck's current level of functioning? Strengths? Weaknesses?
2. What academic problems does Chuck have?
3. Does Chuck have a problem functioning socially? How?
4. What suggestions do you have to help Chuck function comfortably with his age-mates?

UNIT 6
Peer Groups

Case Study 31
Mrs. Brown's Diary

Janet Wilcox is a sixteen-year-old junior who transferred to Walnut High School three weeks after the beginning of the school year. As a result of the transfer, a change in graduation requirements, and several credits that were not accepted from the previous high school, Janet found herself in my freshman English class. The records that had been received from her previous high school did not prepare me for Janet Wilcox: She was a very pretty young woman who was almost six feet tall and slender, was known throughout the area as "the premier talented" volleyball player, and had been a member of the National Honor Society since the sixth grade. Little was known about her family; she refused to discuss anything about them. When pressed for information about her family, she would respond by saying, "It's all in my records, look for yourself!"

Socially, Janet is puzzling. She has made no effort whatsoever to establish any type of communication or rapport with me this year. It is as if she really dislikes me for some reason, which doesn't really bother me; I just don't know why. The only reaction she makes to me is an occasional look of disgust or rolling of the eyes, which irritates me at times. It has been so frustrating teaching when the learner refuses to participate in the learning process. Yesterday, I asked Janet a question, and she looked at me and said, "Are you talking to me or to the window?" Any comments made to her receive similar responses. I have tried cooperative learning, small and large groups; I tried panels, speeches, and reports. I have been unable to gain her interest in anything. She only "goes through the motions" with whatever project is assigned.

Also puzzling to me is Janet's relationship with her classmates. Janet is in a class with thirty-one freshmen, yet she develops "buddy types" of relationships with them. I have had to remind her quite a number of times about whispering and passing notes in class to the freshmen. Not that freshmen are inflicted with a disease or plague and should not be allowed to talk to a junior, but it is rather odd for a junior eagerly to seek the friendship of freshmen. Juniors generally avoid being seen standing next to a freshman, let alone being seen talking to one. Janet's behavior is most puzzling.

Often I notice Janet in the halls and observe the group of students around her. Janet definitely does not hang out with the "in" group; her peer group is on the fringe of being classified as "freaks." They keep to themselves, wear all black clothes and white pancake makeup, and wear sunglasses inside the school. It is difficult for me to believe that Janet actually fits into this social group. Generally, I have observed that Janet doesn't dress like a "preppy"; however, I have never seen her dressed to look like the "night of the living dead" either.

I had a conference with Janet's parents to explain some of the things I had observed and to give them an assessment of Janet's progress in my English class. I informed them that she would be receiving a D in my class. They said little during the conference; and after it was over, her mother said coldly, "Is that all you wanted to say?" I am at my wits end; I don't know what to do. Janet's parents have made it quite clear to me, the principal, and the school board: "Janet is of legal age." She may do exactly what she wants to do. If you don't like what she is doing, that's tough! Don't call us again, unless you are expelling her!"

QUESTIONS

1. Are there any specific actions that Mrs. Brown can do within her class?
2. How can Mrs. Brown involve the entire class? Should she?
3. If you were Mrs. Brown's supervisor, what would you recommend?
4. How can Mrs. Brown help Janet? Should she?

Case Study 32
Three Brothers

Mrs. Jane Collins is an English teacher and the senior class advisor. She is Trevor's homeroom teacher and lives across the street from his family. Preparing for the last semester of the school year, she reflects about Trevor's background. She has discussed his family, its background, individual family members, and the family's future with the principal, fellow teachers, and social workers.

Barry, Trevor, and Larry are the three youngest brothers in a family of five children. They have one older brother, Jack, and the eldest is a sister, Gayle. Gayle is now married and has a son of her own. Jack is a junior at Baker College; he has just been elected the president of his fraternity, Pi Kappa Alpha. Because they are both involved in their own lives, Jack and Gayle rarely see the three boys.

The family began to have tremendous problems shortly after the youngest son, Barry, was born. When Barry reached his third birthday, his parents were divorced. The four boys then lived with their dad; their mother had remarried within two months of the divorce. As a single parent, Brian Jackson had performed admirably, keeping the boys together and making the family work. However, it seemed that when Jack left for college, trouble quickly followed.

Brian's career caused him to be involved frequently with reduction in force; his job depends directly on how the economy is doing. The company for which he worked suddenly fired him after several years of service. Totally unprepared for the blow, he sent the boys to live with their mother and her new husband, Mike. Barry, Trevor, and Larry have always been close, but with this move, they really had to band together. Mike is a dominant, controlling individual. Mike let everyone know that he did not want to be responsible for raising someone else's children, but their mother begged relentlessly to let the boys stay with them. Mike finally agreed to it only when he discovered that he had a source of "cheap" labor for his warehouse business.

Jane Collins had found the three boys to be quite pleasant and easygoing. Larry, the oldest of the three, had sensed that things with Mike weren't very good. He obeyed and submitted to Mike's authority and tried to remain pleasant. At seventeen years of age, he knew he only had to tolerate Mike's abusive nature a few more years; he looked forward to being on his own. Larry's real concern was for his two younger brothers. Mike was also quite abusive to Barry and Trevor. Larry had to intervene in many fights that Mike had with Barry and Trevor.

When they were much younger, Barry and Trevor looked up to Larry when times were tough. Barry had always been easygoing, easy to talk to, and always concerned about the welfare of others. Trevor had the most trouble, constantly rebelling against and regularly questioning Mike's authority. The boys' mother, Marcie, had to get involved regularly and separate Trevor and Mike. Eventually Mike moved out of the house. It was apparent to all that the marriage was in serious trouble. He gave Marcie money to run the household and let her keep her job at the warehouse; however, he would not let the boys work for him and refused to have anything to do with them.

Barry and Trevor are living with various friends for several nights each week. They are never in any household for more than four days. Barry is a sophomore, and Trevor is a senior. Going to school, getting by, and trying to hold a job are the major concerns for the boys. They earn enough money to get by. It appears that Trevor's senior year in school will be stressful.

In Mrs. Collins's English class, Trevor seems to be going through the motions of participating in the class. Mrs. Collins had similar comments from all of his teachers. As she reflects upon his grades, she believes that he has achieved a great deal. Yet his grades are far below the academic standards established by the school district for graduation. If Trevor is to graduate, he must have a remarkable end-of-the-year performance in all of his classes. Mrs. Collins has scheduled a conference with Trevor and his mother on Friday afternoon to discuss the state of graduation for him.

QUESTIONS

1. How would you prepare for the conference on Friday?
2. What specific recommendations would you provide to Trevor's teachers?
3. What is the major problem facing Mrs. Collins?
4. How can the school district become involved?

Case Study 33
A Statement from James Green, Social Studies Teacher

Ernie Jaynes is a seventeen-year-old senior at Omaha Southwest Senior High School; he usually is very involved in school activities, which makes him fairly popular. I have known Ernie for almost three years. He has been in one of my classes as well as being the equipment manager for the athletic team that I coach. Ernie is one of those kids who seems to have too much energy, never knowing what to do with his energy no matter how many things he is given to do. As his homeroom teacher, I am often concerned that Ernie's abundance of energy is going to get directed in the wrong way. He is a good-natured young man and will jump blindly into anything with both feet. These attributes are all very positive, if only Ernie would look before he leaps.

As I said, Ernie is very, very active. Although he is not skilled in other sports, he enjoys wrestling, in which he has been a medalist in a couple of varsity tournaments and maintains about an 80 percent winning percentage. Ernie also maintains a grade point average of 3.85 . He is involved with the Southwest's academic bowl team and the science department's Mind Olympiad team. He regularly travels to various contests and tournaments as a member of both teams. He is active in other club activities, such as the Spanish and German clubs and the National Honor Society.

One would think that with all of this involvement and his studies, Ernie would be fairly well adjusted socially. He does get along well with peers, but others and I have noticed that he can become overbearing. In conversation, he really likes to dominate, making it difficult for others to become involved. He can be rude by interrupting or losing eye contact, gazing off in the distance, or walking away when he is the listener. He is often opinionated and offends his listeners, having little regard for their opinions. When he is engaged in a one-on-one conversation, he has great difficulty in remaining stationary; he is constantly fidgeting, twisting, and looking around. He has trouble standing still.

As I have stated, Ernie is a pretty good kid all around, but he did finally cross the line. He decided to vandalize a newspaper stand one night. He didn't necessarily want the money; he just wanted to pull a prank. (He has hinted that it was part of a "dare" or a challenge but has never said outright what brought about the events.) He put the entire vending machine in the trunk of his car, but the lid to the trunk did not close entirely. On the way home he was stopped by the police and arrested, and spent the night in jail. His parents bailed him out the next day, and they were furious. Ernie tried to play off the incident as "no big deal."

With the advice of his attorney, he planned to plead guilty if the incident would not be placed on his permanent record. The sentence was reduced to a year's probation; any violations would result in this incident's being placed on his permanent record. Ernie thought this would be great, until he found out the restriction of this probation. He has quieted down considerably since the trial, and the probation period has begun.

QUESTIONS

1. If you had been Ernie's teacher, how would you have responded to these events?
2. What is Ernie's current level of functioning?
3. Should any additional penalties be imposed by the school district?
4. As Ernie's homeroom teacher, how can you provide assistance?

Troubled Teenagers

Case Study 34
Mike Is Seventeen Years Old

Mike Smith is a seventeen-year-old junior in Mr. Lawson's sixth period social studies class. Physically, Mike is very well developed, and all of the girls have noticed him. He always seems to have four or five girls sitting around him who describe him as a "hunk." He is always neat and well groomed and looks like he has just returned from a clothing store. He wears the latest fashions that teenagers wear, and he seems to always have money. Once Mr. Lawson saw him at a fast-food restaurant with at least three hundred dollars.

When Mr. Lawson asks Mike about the money and the clothes, he replies, "You know, when you're good, you're good. I'm good and people notice." He does not have any job of which Mr. Lawson is aware. Asked whether his son has a job, Mike's father replied, "What! Mike has never worked at anything. He barely can get dressed for school without help. I cannot imagine Mike working." His father's response was a surprise. No one at school knows if Mike has a job and they support what his father said.

Mike is the product of two broken homes. When his parents were divorced, he went to live with his father. Last year his father was divorced again, and Mike went to live with his father and his father's girlfriend. Mike rarely talks about his family life. Mr. Lawson doesn't think Mike is comfortable with the current arrangements of the family. When Mike was a sophomore, he talk with Mr. Lawson about a lot of the things, and the teacher felt they had developed a close relationship. Since the second divorce, Mike has not talked about anything other than what occurs in the class.

Academically, Mike has been classified as having learning disabilities, and Mr. Lawson believes that Mike is bright enough to convince the special education teacher of his disability. He has noticed that Mike can excel at almost anything he tries. During the social studies class, he writes extremely well. On unit tests and pop quizzes, whether oral or written, Mike excels. He grasps complex concepts extremely well and responds to questions with skill, depth, and critical thought. He is an extremely talented individual. All of the papers he has handed to Mr. Lawson, in class or out of class, are well written and evidence critical thought. He has a terrific memory and great skills in math, science, and languages. The English and reading teachers have assessed his reading as at a superior level. They were surprised when Mike was classified as a student with learning disabilities.

Mike is unpredictable emotionally. He has sudden, dramatic mood swings. Some days when things are going well, Mike is personable, likable, and fun. When his mood darkens, he is the exact opposite. Mike in a dark mood is cold, cruel, vicious, and extremely angry. Mr. Lawson can tell exactly what type of mood Mike is in when he takes attendance at the beginning of the hour. These mood swings can also get Mike into trouble with teachers and students. The other boys in the class appear to admire and respect him, but not during his dark moods.

Yesterday in class, during a panel discussion, Mike abruptly stood up and looked around the class. He singled out one student and pointed at him, and then he told a girl in another part of the room to shut her mouth and stop looking at him. Everyone in the class was shocked at the outburst. At the end of the class, he approached the girl and told her that he really didn't mean it. The girl and her friends were confused by the apology. This is not the first outburst; nor is it the first apology.

Mr. Lawson believes that some of Mike's problems are a result of his parents' divorce. From talking to Mike, the teacher thinks he lives with his mother and one of her boyfriends on the weekends, but he has never explicitly said this. Mike frequently talks about his father, how they do many things together, cutting wood, fishing, and hunting. Mike often comments on how much he values the good relationship they have; it is almost like best friends.

The guidance counselor and the physical education teacher believe that Mike is selling drugs. The students offer a variety of explanations. They don't have any clear reasons for his behavior. Mr. Lawson admits that he is at a loss to explain Mike's recent behavior.

QUESTIONS

1. What is the problem?
2. What suggestions would you make to Mike for handling his mood swings?
3. What teaching strategies would you use with Mike in the social studies class?
4. What changes would you make within the learning environment to help Mike adjust?

Case Study 35
Chris and Gene

Chris is fourteen years old. She is bright, pretty, and talented and has a terrific sense of humor. All of the students in the eighth grade like Chris, and they also respect her talent and abilities. She plays basketball so well that she has attracted national attention. Chris is terrific. She is Mr. Gerber's top math student and exhibits a tremendous amount of confidence and self-esteem. When she enters the room, there is a lot of energy and excitement created. It is like someone turns on an electric switch. Mr. Gerber knows that he shouldn't be this partial to or favor one student, yet this young lady is special to everyone.

Chris has a lot of friends in both the seventh and eighth grades. A majority of the teachers and students believe she is one of the most popular girls in the junior high school. Chris is fourteen years old and is in love for the very first time. Mr. Gerber thinks they make a terrific couple. He and his teaching partner think it is good for both students. They think that both student's parents are pleased also.

Chris is six feet four and one half inches tall. She weighs about one hundred and ninety-six pounds. Her boyfriend, Gene, is four feet eight inches tall and weighs about eighty-five pounds. He is as talented, as witty, and as skilled as Chris; intellectually, they make a terrific couple. They usually hold hands as they walk down the hall together; they appear to enjoy each other a great deal.

OK! What is the problem? The students start early during the first period of the day and continue nonstop until the last period of the day, teasing Chris and Gene about their being so tall and so short. The teasing goes on until either Chris or Gene begins to cry. The crying brings more teasing. It appears that the students at the junior high school enjoy punishing other students for being different.

At first Mr. Gerber did not notice that the teasing had become vicious. He thought the students liked the couple and were ribbing them in a

93

good-natured way. He thought that Chris and Gene were enjoying the teasing. In fact, Mr. Gerber had also participated in the teasing, as had other teachers. Mr. Gerber was wrong. The other teachers were wrong. The students were wrong.

QUESTIONS

1. What is the problem?
2. As the math teacher, what do you do?
3. What do you tell the students in your class?
4. How can you help Chris? Gene? Both?

Case Study 36
Donald

Donald is a fifteen-year-old student in Miss Mullaney's third-period freshman science class. He is a slender boy who is of average height with a slight acne problem. Donald struggled in class during the first semester. He has the ability to be successful, but he did not show any interest in the class. On the first-semester report card, Miss Mullaney indicated that his poor grades were due to a lack of effort, poor test scores, and a bad attitude; Donald flunked science. When Miss Mullaney tried to talk to him about his lack of effort, he seemed to ignore her suggestions and said simply that he would try harder.

After the semester break, Donald's parents took him for professional help. Miss Mullaney was not aware of any emotional problems that Donald had been experiencing: Her assessment was a lack of effort and a poor attitude toward science; Donald's other teachers shared this assessment of his effort for the first grading period. All of the teachers believe that he has ability, but he appears to be quite distracted. Miss Mullaney doesn't think Donald will be one of the top science students, but she does believe that he has the ability to be successful in the class.

According to his parents, Donald was suffering from severe depression. They have indicated that he will be taking medication to help him concentrate and will be seeing a professional on a routine basis. Both parents are pleased to have a solution to Donald's problems.

Miss Mullaney finds it hard to believe that Donald is suffering from severe depression. Of course, she's not a physician; however, she has known Donald, his family, and his friends for the past ten years. She has known Donald to be an average student with average interests and average skills. She cannot believe that any medications will convert him into a superior student.

Throughout the second semester, Donald has walked around the school in a dazed condition. He appears listless, shows no expressions, has a lack of energy, and looks pale. Miss Mullaney has sent notes to the principal and to the parents expressing her concern for Donald. They seemed to be convinced that the medication is the correct approach.

During science class, Donald has great difficulty responding to the simplest questions. When Miss Mullaney places him into small study groups, he sleeps. It is apparent to all that the medication is making him sleepy. He cannot listen, study, and learn when he is asleep. Miss Mullaney has tried to speak with his parents about her observations, but they have ignored all of her comments. The other teachers report similar reactions.

The students in the science class say that Donald was dating Alice Long for three weeks. On a date at the movies, Donald gave her a friendship ring; she gave it back to him and left the movie. The students say that she has avoided him since the date and has been saying unkind things about him. Miss Mullaney doesn't know how true any of this information is, but she knows that Donald had a different attitude after their date.

QUESTIONS

1. What modifications would you make to the learning environment to accommodate Donald's unique learning needs?
2. What strategies would you recommend to Miss Mullaney?
3. Are there behaviors that suggest problems other than learning?

Case Study 37
Alexander Is Sixteen Years Old

Alexander is almost sixteen years old and in the eighth grade. He is one of the students whom a school counselor has described to as being on the "four year plan." This means failing sixth grade twice, failing seventh grade twice, skipping eighth grade, and going on to the ninth grade. However, Alexander has become an exception to that plan; it was decided by his parents, three guidance counselors, teachers at the high school and the junior high school, the assistant principal, and the principal that Alexander should stay in junior high school for the eighth grade and not be permitted to go to the ninth grade. They decided that he was not mature enough to survive in the high school environment. None of Alexander's family offer support for him. Many teachers at the junior and senior high school have said that he would be "eaten alive" by the high school crowd. If he were allowed to go to the high school this year, everyone believes he would drop out of school within a few months.

Currently, he is passing his social studies class with a C. His math teacher stated that she is frustrated with Alexander. He has spent two years in a seventh-grade math class, yet he still cannot do the level of math required of the seventh-graders. Last year as a seventh-grader, Alexander would work well one day and not do anything for the next two or three days. He would ask questions, ask for help, seem to understand the concepts, and yet not seem to retain any of the information. The pattern continues for this year, and he is failing the math class again. Alexander is sixteen years old and has been in the same math class for three years.

Alexander is a puzzle to all of the teachers at the junior high school. In all of his classes, it is the same; his academic performance is very inconsistent. No teacher has an explanation or a solution to Alexander's problems. The special education teacher obtained permission from his parents to have Alexander evaluated. The evaluation revealed that his performance fell within a normal range of abilities. The special education teacher said there was no evidence of learning disabilities, nor physical or heredity problems.

He really doesn't belong with the other junior high school students. He is almost a foot taller and physically more mature than all of the other students, and socially is three years behind all of them. When Alexander is walking down the hall, it is easy to spot him, as he is the tallest, largest, and loudest of the students.

In the classroom, Alexander does not appear unusual outside of his being older than the others. Generally, he is quiet, speaks when spoken to, and respects his teachers. Outside before school, in the hallways, in the cafeteria, or on the school bus, he is loud, aggressive, and threatening to the other students.

Alexander is the youngest in a family of four. The family appears to be indifferent about doing things together. None of the teachers can remember seeing the family at any of the school activities. None of the other members of the family have completed their high school education; all left the school before finishing the eleventh grade.

QUESTIONS

1. What strategies should the math teacher use to meet Alexander's needs?
2. What learning problems does Alexander exhibit?
3. If Alexander was in your math class, what would be your focus?
4. What is the problem?

Case Study 38
Mary Bright

Mrs. Alvarez heard about Mary Bright before she actually encountered her in her English class. Mary is the library assistant from the seventh grade. She works in the library during the fourth and fifth periods. The librarian, Kate, seems to have chosen Mary as her special project for the year. Kate was acquainted with Mary at the elementary school. While Mary was at the elementary school, she was bright and witty, had a terrific sense of humor, was very athletic, and, as Kate said, was a "real people person."

It is the first grading period, and Mrs. Alvarez can hardly believe that Mary is the same person Kate described. She has missed a great deal of school and constantly avoided contact with other students during the first months of the school year. None of Mary's friends have been able to explain her behavior. She will not eat lunch in the cafeteria with other students, preferring to bring lunch to the library to eat alone. During a seventh-grade class meeting, Mrs. Alvarez noticed that Mary sat in the back of the classroom; after several minutes, she noticed that she had moved into a corner. She was pressed into the corner, as if she was trying blend into the wall.

Kate has noticed that Mary brings food for lunch; however, Kate has never witnessed Mary eating. The librarian theorizes that Mary is terrified of other people and this has caused most of the problems. Kate believes that with more social opportunities Mary will overcome her apparent shyness.

Mrs. Alvarez was unsure how Mary would respond in her class, since her teaching style includes class discussion, small group work, and peer editing of writing. Her classroom behavior is not surprising. She is quiet and rarely alters her facial expressions. Mrs. Alvarez finds it impossible to get Mary to speak in the classroom, no matter what activities she designs. Instead she will motion, gesture, or sit and say nothing. Over the past two weeks, Mrs. Alvarez has noticed that for a fourteen-year-old girl, she appears pale and sickly. When called on for an answer to a discussion question, she answers in a voice so faint she can hardly be heard. During small groups, she remains quiet. However, when another student speaks to her (usually with reference to her shyness), she often shows a faint smile.

The interesting thing is that when given the opportunity, Mary writes lengthy stories and personal reflections with no hesitation about subject or emotional impact. It's almost as if she opens a floodgate when she writes, and all the bottled-up expression pours onto the paper.

Knowing Mary through personal contact, one might get the impression that she is a shy and unhappy person. Knowing Mary through her writing suggests the opposite. She expresses the same interests, desires, and needs as any other girl her age.

QUESTIONS

1. What is the problem?
2. If you were Mrs. Alvarez, what could you do to meet her needs?
3. How can the librarian provide help to Mary?
4. What role should Mrs. Alvarez perform?

Case Study 39
Mrs. Thompson's Report on Jackie

There is no polite way to say it. The girls in my second-period physical education class believe Jackie is an abuser. Jackie is fourteen years old, but he is not a typical fourteen-year-old freshman boy. He is about six feet tall, weighs about one hundred and ninety pounds, is very handsome, and has a vulgar vocabulary. It seems that every other word he uses is an obscene word, reference to a body function, or proposition. Any girl who is unfortunate enough to be standing near him is likely to be pinched, patted, hit, slapped, or obscenely grabbed. He has terrified and terrorized all the females and I include myself among them. I too have experienced what his father has described as "harmless pranks that boys play to show they are boys." Jackie, the principal, the guidance counselor, Jackie's parents, and an attorney from the board of education have met several times since the beginning of the year.

Jackie has been at the junior high school for almost two months, having transferred at the beginning of the school year. The family moved into the area from a town in another state and there were no records present when he registered for school. Since that time, the school has received his grades and some rather disturbing news. His records indicate nothing about any of the behavior he is now showing toward the girls and women at the school.

Today was not my best day for teaching at the junior high school. I lost my temper in front of a class of ninth-grade students. I said a lot of things that I should not have said to a student. I touched a student in a manner that I never have done in my twelve years of teaching. I acted more like one of the students than an experienced teacher. The reasons for my behavior are not enough to justify what I did. I did not react in a professional manner.

The second-period physical education class began as it always does at the beginning of the school year. Students, especially the girls, are consistently late getting into the dressing rooms, getting changed into their uniforms, and getting out onto the gym floor ready for the class. For two weeks in a row, I have reminded the girls to be considerate of the other members of the class and be ready for the class on time.

There are about thirty-five students in this class. As the tardy bell rang, there was a flurry of activity, and then silence for about six minutes. The boys were in their dressing room, and the girls were in theirs. I and my assistant, Mr. Drake, were standing in the middle of the gym floor, waiting for the students to begin to emerge from the dressing rooms.

Suddenly, there was a loud, shrill scream coming from the girls dressing room. It was followed by a chorus of screams and yells. I rushed into the dressing room with Mr. Drake standing by the door. When I entered the room, I saw Jackie standing in a corner with a camera, taking pictures of the girls dressing. He was laughing uproariously. I was furious. I grabbed him by his shirt collar and escorted him from the dressing room. Mr. Drake and I took him to the principal's office.

QUESTIONS

1. What do you do?
2. If you were Mrs. Thompson, what would you tell the girls in your phys ed class?
3. What do you say to Jackie?
4. What precautions should you take?

Case Study 40
Micah

Micah Bowles is an alcoholic. Micah is a high school senior out of control. He is also the only child of the community's only physician. Dr. Bowles is the chair of the local board of education, and has been active in all aspects of the school environment. He provides a generous donation for two teachers each year to pursue graduate study. Dr. Bowles is well liked and well respected throughout the community.

This is Miss Norris's first year teaching math at the high school. She has Micah in her fourth period. The math class is after the lunch period, when Micah has had more to drink. Miss Norris had a successful first grading period and she believes the students, parents, and school administration respect her and her abilities. The students respond positively to her teaching, coaching, and conference skills. Many parents have visited her classroom, and all have made positive comments about her to the principal and board members. Miss Norris respects Dr. Bowles; however, she thinks Micah Bowles is a loud, abusive drunk.

She dreads teaching the fourth-period math class, because Micah will be in the class, drunk again. He either will sleep or will be loud and abusive. His abusive behavior involves nasty comments to students, sexual harassment, and rude and crude comments to Miss Norris. All the students in the class know that Micah drinks throughout the day, but he drinks more at lunch than at any other time. Miss Norris's problem is that he is in her class after he has been drinking.

Miss Norris's feels intimidated by Micah. What does she say to his parents? What does she say to him? She is only twenty-two years old, and he is eighteen years old. Physically, he is bigger than her. She is only five feet tall and finds him very threatening. Micah smells of alcohol no matter what cologne he uses to cover it.

Micah is a talented athlete, with many college recruiters visiting him every week, a bright student with a lot of potential, and a drunk. Miss Norris believes that Micah is not the only student involved with drinking; however, she cannot prove it. She doesn't want to sound like she's on a crusade to abolish alcohol; she believes it should be the decision of a responsible adult. Micah is eighteen years old, but Miss Norris is not sure that he is acting very responsibly.

As Micah's math teacher, she has tried to talk with him on numerous occasions, but with little success. He does not respond positively to anything she suggests. He does superior work on all of her tests and seems to understand the concepts she has taught. The problem seems to be a matter of respect. Miss Norris doesn't think Micah has very much respect for her or her opinions. He has hinted on several occasions that his father is Miss Norris's "boss." He also has suggested that he likes to talk with his father about different courses. On parents' night, Mrs. Bowles said hello and quickly left Miss Norris's classroom; she made no comments about Micah or his grades.

The students in the fourth-period math class generally respect Micah's many accomplishments both as an athlete and in academics. Miss Norris is not sure that all of the students like Micah, but they don't seem to generally dislike him, either. She thinks they see him as someone with power and influence.

From what she has been able to discover, Miss Norris thinks Micah has been an alcoholic for almost three years. He has had many problems with the local law enforcement; because of Dr. Bowles's reputation, Micah has been permitted to do anything.

QUESTIONS

1. What is the first thing Miss Norris should do?
2. What should Miss Norris say to Micah? Should she make any comment?
3. What should Miss Norris say to the parents? Should the principal be involved?
4. How should she approach any fears of physical intimidation?

Case Study 41
Connie

Connie is a fourteen-year-old eighth-grader. Her family consists of her parents, who both work, and a sister, Diane, who is five years older. Diane did everything for Connie as the two were growing up. When the school year began last month, it was apparent to everyone that Connie missed Diane. Without Diane to support her and ensure that she understood her assignments, Connie has been struggling in all of her classes. She walks around in a dark mood that keeps everyone at a distance. She rarely smiles or speaks to anyone. If spoken to, she usually gives a single-word response. This has been a difficult time for her.

Connie is in Mr. Compton's second-period social studies class at the junior high school. He has spoken with her, Diane, and both of their parents. Diane and her parents think Connie needs more time to adjust to the new change. He tries to be receptive and open-minded, but he doesn't think this is the problem. He believes that Connie has more severe problems than he is capable of handling. He doesn't feel adequately prepared to deal with this in his classroom.

After the meeting with the family, the teachers, and the school administration, there was a feeling of relief by everyone. Mr. Compton thinks that although they talked about some issues, they did not deal with the problem. Connie is not adjusting to having to rely on herself. She is not addressing anything that has been brought to her attention. During the conference, her mother tried to get Connie to talk about anything that was bothering her, but Connie refused to participate in any of the conversation even when asked direct questions. Mr. Compton felt uneasy, seeing her look withdrawn, depressed, and isolated.

Today, during the social studies class, Mr. Compton asked his students to work on class projects within their cooperative groups. After ten minutes, he noticed that the girls in Connie's group were talking freely with each other, but Connie was staring out into space. He spoke to her several times, but she did not respond. Concerned, he called the school nurse. When the nurse entered the classroom and spoke, Connie jumped with a start. When Connie recognized who it was, she stood up, began to cry, and screamed in a loud voice. It was eerie. The students in the class became completely silent. Mr. Compton, nervous, didn't know what to do or say.

When the nurse escorted Connie out the classroom and to the principal's office, the talk of the day at the junior high school was about what had happened in second-period social studies. Mr. Compton was not prepared for this type of reaction. Nothing in his training or six years of teaching had prepared him for this. He's tried to talk with the school counselor, but it is hard to described the feelings. All of the students at the junior high school know what happened in his second period social studies class.

It has been almost five weeks since the scene in the classroom and Connie is scheduled to return to school on Monday. Mr. Compton isn't sure what to do. He has spoken to the principal, who says to treat her in as a normal a manner as possible. The school counselor says that she will be available to talk to the class; she has been involved with the class since the incident. The students are very nervous about Connie's return to class, and almost all of them have expressed their concern about her returning to school.

QUESTIONS

1. What should Mr. Compton tell the class? Should he address the class?
2. How should Mr. Compton react to Connie?
3. How should the school counselor be involved in the class?
4. How should the class routine be altered to adjust to Connie's unique needs?

Case Study 42
The Diaries of Andy and Mrs. Green

MRS. GREEN

Andy is a sixteen-year-old tenth-grader who struggles socially, economically, physically, and academically. I know Andy only from observing him in my tenth-grade English class. He has been in my class for the past four months; during this period of time, he has had to overcome so many problems. During my ten years of teaching, I cannot recall any student having these problems. I've tried to maintain a very professional relationship with Andy, yet I want him to know that I am interested in him as an individual. I've kept him after class and after school to help him.

ANDY

My family—that's my ten-year-old sister, me, and my dad—lives in an apartment two blocks from the school. My parents were divorced last year; it's so hard not to have mom to talk to, to push me, to tease me, or to laugh at my silly jokes. I miss her a lot, and my dad and I are not very close. I love him, but he works so hard, is tired a lot, and doesn't have very much time for me. Mrs. Green drives me crazy; she is such a nosy teacher. I study hard for her English class, but English is hard for me. What I want to know is, Do people really talk like those people in *Julius Caesar?* I'm never going to use this stuff, so why are we having to read stuff by these ancient people? I don't think that she likes me. She always asks such personal questions. Yesterday, she wanted to know why I didn't have any girlfriends.

MRS. GREEN

I've tried to make Andy feel that he is a part of the class. His parents were divorced last year, which was very difficult for everyone. Andy's mother and her family had financial security before the marriage; I think Andy's father spent all of the money that she had inherited on foolish spending. I always thought that she had married far out of her social class.

ANDY

During English class, Mrs. Green always points out my writing or speaking mistakes to the whole class. Yesterday, I wanted to commit suicide; she told Cindi that I was "obscenely eyeing" her. I like Cindi; she's cute, pretty, kind, sweet, and nice to me. I have never said anything to Cindi, because I am too afraid to. I'm so ugly, and she is so pretty.

MRS. GREEN

Andy has some type of physical problem, as he is always slouching in his desk. I have never seen him sit erect like the other boys in the class. His clothes seem so dirty, so wrinkled, and so mismatched. I think the clothes are because of the family's financial situation. I have noticed that Andy has been looking at girls. I think his father should have had a talk with him a long time ago. Socially, he tries to talk with girls who are so far out of his reach. Every time he does these things in my class, I always remind him of them. Since his mother is not at home, I feel that someone has to let him know what he does.

ANDY

Mrs. Day, my history teacher, said today that I have a good chance of making the B honor roll for the second grading period. She said that I had to have a good grade in the English class with Mrs. Green. When I told Mrs. Green about the honor roll, she told me that she didn't see how anyone in the special classes could make the honor roll. I think that was supposed to be an insult, but I'm not sure. I know that I'm not the brightest student, but I do know that I have never been in a special education class. I have trouble understanding English. Does this make me stupid?

MRS. GREEN

Andy asked me about his grade in English for this grading period. I tried to tell him in a very nice way he did not have any ability. Sometimes teachers must be able to tell students that they lack ability rather than trying to mislead them. Andy has some learning problems, and I think they are related to what he inherited from his father.

ANDY

I just talked with Mrs. Green. I feel so stupid, so worthless. Is there anyone anywhere who likes me?

MRS. GREEN

I had to tell Andy that he had to stay after school today to work on his writing. I probably shouldn't devote so much time trying to help him, yet I feel that I have to provide support since his mother is not there for him.

ANDY

What can I say? Mrs. Green has kept me after school again. I feel so trapped. I don't know what to do. There is no one with whom I can talk. I'd like to talk with Mrs. Day, but there are so many students in class there isn't any chance. I probably deserve it.

QUESTIONS

1. What is the problem?
2. If you were Mrs. Day, what would you do?
3. If you were Andy's homeroom teacher, what would you say to Andy?

UNIT 8
Troubled Young Adults

Case Study 43
James

James Caulkin is a junior at Murphey Central High School. Academically, he is a below-average student with an ambition to finish high school and get a job at the local tire company. The process of education has been a mystery for James, and his teachers have described him as "academically at-risk and [walking] around as if in a fog."

Doug Allen, a fifty-year-old bachelor, became the legal guardian when James was fourteen. James's parents had been killed in a car accident; Doug is the only relative. At first Doug resented having to provide for James and to monitor the actions of a teenager. Eventually, both James and Doug reached a point of agreement, and they have enjoyed an uneasy peace since James's fifteenth birthday to the present.

At the beginning of the school year, James and Alice became engaged and married within a week's time. It was quite a lot of stress for Doug; he was unprepared for James. He now was responsible for both James and Alice, who are both seventeen. There had been numerous disagreements between James and Doug. The arguments were about the same topic, money. Alice worked at a local restaurant, while James worked at a fast-food restaurant. James resents having to live with Doug and to depend on his uncle for money. James has a very high frustration level, and his friends describe him as a "powder keg."

James and Alice are in Mrs. Kendrick's first period math class. Mrs. Kendrick has taught at Murphey High School for almost ten years. She has known both James and Alice for about seven years. Mrs. Kendrick has been supportive of James as he works on a speech problem. James is physically immature for a seventeen-year-old, and his stuttering only brings attention to his lack of physical development.

It's Monday morning. Mrs. Kendrick has finished the morning attendance report. As she begins the morning lesson, she notices that James and

Alice are involved in an argument that involves several students around them. Alice is supporting James's position while he is trying to make his point clearly. Everyone in the class is enjoying the chaotic scene, as James becomes more frustrated and stutters more. The noise from the argument begins to take over the classroom.

Mrs. Kendrick leaves the front of the classroom and approaches James. In a firm tone, she tells the class to be quiet and repeats the command to James. He does not respond to her; instead, he yells, points at her, and begins to direct his anger toward her. She is surprised by his tone, his actions, and the physical motions toward her. Alice stands up and demands that everyone listen to James. The noise and actions of the students in the classroom are becoming threatening. Several students near the door have left the classroom. Almost all of the students now are standing.

QUESTIONS

1. What should Mrs. Kendrick do to "defuse" the situation?
2. Could Mrs. Kendrick have anticipated this?
3. After the crisis has been resolved, what should Mrs. Kendrick say to the class?

Case Study 44
Mary Jenkins

Mary Jenkins is a sixteen-year-old sophomore at the high school. She has been to the local health clinic, where she has been told that she is two months pregnant. Upon returning home, she tells her parents what the physician has told her. They were furious; they packed a box of clothes for her and told her never to return. They had spent considerable time telling her how worthless they believed her to be.

Mary is now four months pregnant, and she has spent two months living with various friends. She now is living in a cardboard box in an alley. She has tried to attend school, but it does not seem to be worth the effort. Mary is an average student who has had to work hard to achieve average grades. Learning for Mary has been a difficult task. She has great difficulty reading, math is a mystery for her, and science is far too difficult for her to be concerned with it.

Jean Kelly is a tenth-grade social studies teacher at the high school. She had developed a close relationship with Mary during the past year. After consulting with many local officials, Mary's parents, and the school district, Jean Kelly had assumed the guardianship of Mary. The arrangement between Jean and Mary has lasted for about two months. Mary has become very comfortable with the living arrangement and has begun to make some progress at the high school. Mary is in a social studies class taught by Jean Kelly's best friend, Kathleen.

Wednesday has begun slowly for the social studies class. Kathleen has assigned a group project for the class. The class quickly divides into groups, four students in each, and begins to work on the assignment. Two students in a group beside Mary's group make comments about Mary's physical appearance. At first, the comments are general, but as the class period continues, the comments are directed at her being an unwed mother. The comments are made so that only a few members of the group can hear them. The class has been working on the assignment for almost twenty minutes. Kathleen has been moving about the class, monitoring the progress of the individual groups. She has been listening as well as commenting upon ideas made by individual students.

Kathleen is on one side of the class when she hears a loud scream. Mary has stood up and is trying to make her way to one of the students in another group. She's yelling what she is going to do to the two girls. They stand also but begin to move away from her. The class suddenly erupts with a lot of yelling, pushing, and scuffling.

QUESTIONS

1. What is Kathleen's first responsibility?
2. Since Kathleen is on the opposite side of the classroom, how does she regain control of the class?
3. Does Mary's pregnancy add further responsibility to Kathleen's classroom management?

Case Study 45
Neal

Life has been cruel to Neal, a seventeen-year-old sophomore. Kate, his sister, appeared to have everything that she needed to make her life complete. Neal and his father always had been very close; they went to sport contests, camping, and hunting together. Although Neal had developed a very close relationship with his father, he had never been able to establish the same type of relationship with his mother. His mother and he fought almost all of the time; she wanted him to be something that he could not be. Identifying that ideal was much of the problem for Neal; he couldn't understand what she wanted from him. Neal and Kate, as brother and sister, tolerate each other. Kate wanted a relationship with Neal similar to what she and her mother had developed. The four members of the family rarely did things together. Each pair of the family enjoyed doing things apart from the other pair—Neal and his father, Kate and her mother.

During the summer, his father was murdered. Neal had been at a summer camp fifty miles from his home. Following a trip to the neighboring town, his father was reported by his mother to the local sheriff as missing; he had been missing for a couple of days. Four days after the report, he was found beside the road; he had been murdered apparently for his car and the money that he had carried.

The school year before the murder, Neal came to school like most freshmen. He was afraid and intimidated by everything and everyone that he saw at school. He was starting at a new school with new students and new teachers. He was tall and slender, wore wire-rimmed glasses, and turned bright red when anyone addressed him. Academically, he was a superior student, so he was placed in the advanced classes program. Unfortunately for Neal, this caused him to be labeled as special, a "nerd." He had worn his hair combed straight back with quite a bit of mousse in it. His clothes, although very clean and neat, were plain in color; it did not appear that anything was out of place.

He was particularly obsessive with the neatness of his appearance. In class, he always sat in the front of the room, clearly focused on what was being said by the teacher as well as the other students; he was constantly taking notes on what the teacher was saying. Academically, he was one of the top three or four students in the freshman class of the school.

Neal always had been very shy, so he rarely asked many questions. As far as girls were concerned, he was invisible; they never noticed him no matter what he did. He had a number of male friends that he would talk to, but he rarely initiated any conversations with them. However, they seemed to enjoy his companionship and eagerly sought him out to talk and laugh with him. He appeared to be very happy within this group. In physical education class, it is quite easy to tell that he is not very athletic. He would trip himself and fall frequently to the great delight of his friends. He would take the teasing very good naturedly.

It has been almost a month since the beginning of school; Neal appears to be walking around in a daze. When his father was murdered, Neal missed only a few days of school; his sister, Kate, missed almost three weeks. When he arrived at school, he was very different.

Now he combs his hair on the side if he combs it at all. He sits in the back of the class leaning on the back of his desk with his chin in the palm of his hands. He appears to be listening to what is being said; however, when asked questions about the material, he shrugs his shoulders and refuses to answer. Neal doesn't talk to anyone about anything. When asked by his teachers to talk, he ignores them; when in the school counselor's office, he refuses to answer any questions. After having sat in the counselor's office for about five minutes, he abruptly gets up and goes back to his class. His grades in all subjects are acceptable, but they are not at the same level as they were during his freshman year. In physical education class, he doesn't participate. He seems distant and alienated from any of the groups of students.

All of the students know of his situation and they want to help him. None of his friends or classmates have been able to reach him. If they try to engage him in conversation, he either ignores them or simply walks away. He appears to be a walking robot; he reacts or notices very little about the other students. Many of the students say that he is frightening to them; they want to run away when he enters a class. They don't know how to talk to him or what to talk about. They are very concerned about his behavior at school, on the bus, and at home. Neal's teachers have similar feelings to those of the rest of the students. They don't know what to do; therefore, they work at trying to keep him on task.

No one seems to know how Neal is handling the whole situation. He says nothing to anyone. When the principal, the counselor, the family's pastor, and several teachers had asked his mother about Neal and his performance, she responded rather strangely.

"Is he acting smart to anyone?"

"Is he misbehaving?"

"Has he been late for school?"

"Has there been any trouble at school or on the bus?"

"If Neal has done nothing, then leave him alone. You know this is none of your business. Why don't you take care of the things at school and I will take care of the things at home. If you don't have anything else to say to me, then leave me and my family alone!" It has now been over a month, and the "new" Neal seems the same. Everyone is still concerned.

QUESTIONS

1. What circumstances are causing Neal to react in the manner described?
2. How can the school provide help for Neal? Should the school/ school district attempt to provide help to him?
3. Is the mother right? Why does the school have an obligation to Neal and his family ?
4. What can Neal's friends do?

Case Study 46
Benjamin and Cathy

Benjamin and Cathy have been dating for almost a year. They met at one of the school-sponsored Friday Night Dance-a-Thons. It seemed to Cathy that it was a miracle. They had danced together for one dance; from that moment, Cathy knew that Benjamin was the only boy for her. Benjamin was bright, handsome, witty, and popular and treated her with great respect. No one had treated her like this; he had treated her like a "lady." When she was around her friends, they praised her for her choice. They were constantly telling her how lucky she was to have a boy like Benjamin.

Cathy's academic performance in the classroom was average. She did the class assignments, answered questions, spoke when spoken to, and enjoyed her time in the classroom. Cathy enjoyed school. She always had made friends quickly and seemed to enjoy their companionship. She never had trouble with anyone or anything at school. Her mother was quite proud of Cathy's performance at school.

Being a single parent, Cathy's mother did not like to go to school to deal with Cathy's problems. Her mother often told her, "Your job is to go to school and learn. My job is to work and make the money for us. You do your job and I'll do mine and we'll get along fine. The work at the hospital is long and hard; I can do it only if you do yours." Her mother occasionally dated their neighbor; the three of them would go to the movies and dinner together. Cathy enjoyed being included with her mother's dates; she would dress for the event and felt very much like an adult.

Benjamin was the oldest child in a family of four children. Both of his parents worked in the local factory on the second shift. They usually went to work just as the children came home from school. They had always trusted Benjamin to do what was right. He always had behaved responsibly at home. He had seemed to enjoy caring for his younger brother and sisters; they respected and admired him. On the weekends and on their vacation, the family had taken many trips together.

Saturday night was the turning point for everyone. Benjamin's father received an emergency telephone call from the hospital asking for his permission to perform surgery on his son. Benjamin and the boys in his group had been in a fight with another rival group. Several of the boys had been killed and fifteen or more were severely injured. The police estimated that there were almost sixty boys involved in the fight. The police had been told that Benjamin was the leader of one of the groups; they were waiting to question him. Since Benjamin was eighteen, the police were going to treat him as an adult.

A friend called Cathy's mother to describe an unusual situation. It seemed that there had been a war between two of the local gangs. The hospital was filling up quickly with patients and the ward might need her to work an additional shift. There was an injured boy, Benjamin, who kept calling for a girl named Cathy. She knew that this could not be the same girl, for Cathy was only twelve.

QUESTIONS

1. If you were the mother, how would you handle this situation?
2. How do you prepare the class for the results of the relationship between Benjamin and Cathy? Between Cathy and her mother? Between Benjamin and his father?
3. How can the classroom teacher provide group discussions to deal with this type of relationship?
4. As Cathy's teacher, how do you help her deal with the situation at school?

Case Study 47
Rebecca

Rebecca could be described by her peers as a student who was conscientious, dedicated and hardworking, and yet loved to relax and enjoy her friends. At sixteen years old, she had developed physically, socially, and psychologically as expected; there had been no traumas during this period of her life. Rebecca loved her parents, her two sisters, and what she had planned for her future. Anyone outside the Hughes family would describe her as a young adult who knew exactly what she wanted to do to be successful.

Rebecca told her mother and both sisters that being sixteen years old was a wonderful period in her life. She has been seeing Donnie Suttles for almost two months; her friends referred to this arrangement as dating, but Rebecca and Donnie said only that they were friends. They would drive into the countryside, hike in the mountains, swim together. Donnie, an eighteen-year-old boy, was planning to work with his father in the family's business after graduation. Donnie was looking forward to a life after high school; he, like Rebecca, was regarded by his friends as a happy, hardworking, and likable person. Donnie and his brother liked being brothers, and they enjoyed each other's company.

When Rebecca and Donnie began dating, neither had ever dated regularly or had any serious relationships. They were unaware of the complications of dating. Neither had had sexual relations; they both has wanted to save the sexual act for marriage. They has repeated their beliefs to family members and friends, and it was accepted by everyone that Rebecca and Donnie would remain chaste until their wedding.

Both families and friends can identify the exact week when Rebecca and Donnie began to exhibit behavior completely different from their normal pattern. Both were extremely moody and secretive and appeared quite upset. They refused any attempts by friends and family to discuss anything wrong.

Donnie and Rebecca liked and trusted Mrs. Jodi Kearns, the sophomore home room teacher at the high school. They thought she was wise and compassionate. Many of the students in the high school had mentioned to Donnie and Rebecca that they had gone to her to talk about their serious problems. Mrs. Kearns has earned a reputation as being honest, trustworthy, and reliable.

On Friday after at 4:00 P.M., Donnie and Rebecca entered Mrs. Kearns's classroom and asked to talk with her in private; the fall break for the high school was scheduled to begin the following Monday. Mrs. Kearns wasn't sure what the problem was, but she knew it must be serious.

Without much delay, Rebecca said, "I'm pregnant!"

Mrs. Kearns said, "Have you told your parents?"

"No! How can we do it?" Donnie said. "They will be so hurt."

"We didn't know what to do. We didn't know who to talk to, we thought you would be able to help us. Please?"

QUESTIONS

1. If you were Mrs. Kearns, how would you handle this situation?
2. As a classroom teacher, what are your responsibilities to the teenagers?
3. How can the classroom teacher provide group discussions to deal with this type relationship?
4. As Rebecca's teacher, how do you help her deal with the situation?

Poverty

Case Study 48
A Student's New Personality

Ms. Holtz Delaney began her second year of teaching at the rural grammar school with a great deal of enthusiasm. She had lived in this area for most of her life; she knew all of the parents and families of the children who were in her class. Being relatively small, the school had only kindergarten through the fifth grades. Agriculture was the most important industry in the area. With twenty-two children in her second-grade class, she had heard many and varied stories about living on a farm and working in the fields during the summer and fall. It had seemed like a natural part of her life.

Nothing in all of her teacher education courses prepared her for the "new" little Mary. Mary was now nine years old, bright, talkative, cute, and so friendly. Mary had been in her first-grade class almost a year and a half ago. At that time, she had arrived during the last two months of the school year. Ms. Delaney remembered her as being so quiet, so bright, and possessing so much potential that she had encouraged Mary at every opportunity. By the end of the school year, Mary had demonstrated tremendous progress in her reading, language, speech, and general social skills. Ms. Delaney encouraged Mary, and it had resulted in a rapid, individual development.

It was apparent to Ms. Delaney that Mary had made many discoveries since she had last seen her. In fact, in her casual speech, Mary used such vulgar language and so many swear words that Ms. Delaney had difficulty concentrating on what Mary said to her. After a meeting with Mary, Ms. Delaney commented to the principal, "It was amazing to observe that such language would be coming from a child so innocent in appearance and at such a young age."

For four days in a row, Mary wore the same clothing which appeared not to have been washed. After the fourth day, Ms. Delaney located several appropriate dresses and gave them to Mary. She eagerly accepted them and thanked Ms. Delaney. The next day, Mary wore the same outfit she had worn on the previous days. It had been difficult to determine which was more embarrassing to Ms. Delaney and to other members of the class—Mary's vulgar language, her clothing, or her refusal to wear underwear. It wasn't only that she did not wear underwear; Mary seemed to take great delight in showing other children that she did not. The principal, the school nurse, and Ms. Delaney had talked with Mary about the underwear and the language for five days in a row with no progress.

Mary's parents were migrant workers who arrived in the area to pick the spring crop of green beans; this meant that they would be in the area for about two months and then would move on to the next field. Mary's parents left very early in the morning and did not return until late at night. They generally worked six to seven days a week; obviously, they had little time to spend with Mary. They expected her to entertain herself and create as few disturbances as possible. Mary rarely saw her parents except when they were traveling from one site to another. Ms. Delaney had tried often to arrange conferences with the parents; however, they never returned her notes. When she made a home visit, they would be embarrassed by her presence and say little to her. Communication with Mary's parents was almost nonexistent, no matter what Ms. Delaney tried. From conversations with her, Ms. Delaney determined that Mary had been in at least fifteen schools during the past year and a half.

Ms. Delaney felt quite uncomfortable with Mary's new personality. This "new personality" made Ms. Delaney feel sad and helpless. Mary had learned to make friends quickly by developing a quick wit and personality that was entertaining to people she did not know. If she did not make friends quickly, she would have no one with whom to play or talk. She did not have to be concerned with long-term relationships, because she and her family rarely were in one place longer than seven weeks.

QUESTIONS

1. How can Ms. Delaney help Mary? Should she?
2. How can the curriculum be altered to provide positive role models for Mary?
3. What specific things can Ms. Delaney do to help Mary with her language?
4. How can Ms. Delaney help the other children to understand Mary?
5. What survival skills can Mrs. Delaney teach Mary?

Case Study 49
David

David is a twelve-year-old boy who lives in a small, two-bedroom trailer with his parents, his brother, Robert, who is ten years old, and his sister, Susan, who is nine. It is a new year at school; David is enjoying his first week of being in Mrs. King's sixth-grade class. Mrs. King and David have known each other since he was in her first-grade class. He always had liked her and had enjoyed her class. She had made many special efforts to encourage him since that time. Quite often she would invite him over to her house to eat dinner with her and her family. After school or on Saturday, David would mow the lawn at her house or do other odd jobs. This was a way that he could earn the money that he needed for school.

David made the adjustment to junior high school quite easily; he usually made friends quickly. He seemed to enjoy school and all of the activity that occurred there. Since he knew the members of his class, the first week of school was an enjoyable time for him. He was an average student that worked very hard to achieve modest successes. All of his teachers noticed his willingness to follow directions and cooperate in all of the classroom activities. He was always polite and very well mannered.

Mrs. King was introduced to David and his parents by a social worker almost six years ago. Mrs. King had worked with the county's nutrition program for the summer and had devoted several months working with this family. From this vantage point, Mrs. King believed that the family had made much progress since that time. The father has been restricted to a wheelchair; he lost his legs during a railroad accident almost ten years ago. The mother is mentally handicapped but works quite hard to care for the family.

Frequently, David would miss school so that he could work at some job to earn money for the family. During his fifth-grade year, the social worker had to visit David and his parents almost every other week to remind them that David had to go to school. This was one of the most unpleasant tasks for the social worker to do. She understood why David had to work and why he had to miss school, yet if he didn't go to school, the family, specifically David, would be destined to repeat the cycle of poverty. On the weekly visits, everyone would agree to do better, yet by the next day, David was repeating his pattern of absence.

On the first day of his sixth-grade session, Mrs. King and David met to discuss what the new year was going to be. She outlined the courses that he had to take at the junior high school and what his responsibilities were going to be. David had promised to attend school regularly; however, Mrs. King reminded him that he had promised that each year. David promised that he would do much better in school. Following the meeting with David, Mrs. King and two of the trade instructors met to arrange a placement for David on a part-time basis. The principal, the instructors, Mrs. King, and the father met the following Friday to work out the details of David's instructional time and his work schedule. It appeared that everyone was happy with all of the arrangements. On the following Friday afternoon, David would begin his new assignments.

On Thursday and Friday, David was absent from school. He had accepted a job at one of the local warehouses; he worked two days a week from four to midnight on Thursday and Friday. David explained to Mrs. King that he did not have clothing and shoes to wear to school and that he had to earn the money to buy these things. He told her that going to junior high school was more expensive for him than he had anticipated.

QUESTIONS

1. What changes are needed in the curriculum to provide David with the critical information and skills that he needs?
2. What is David's current level of development?
3. If you were Mrs. King, what specific things would you do to help David and his family?
4. How are David's needs being met within the classroom setting?

Case Study 50
Three Sisters

Janice, who is twelve, Jewel, who is fourteen, and Jaylene, who is sixteen, live with their parents in a room in a warehouse in the city. They have lived in the one large room for almost two years. The school they occasionally attended was two blocks from their house. The girls have presented many unique situations for the local school administration and the school board. The girls maintain steady boyfriends that they visit often when the parents are not present. The lives of the girls at home may be generously described as "volatile." A social worker visits the family every two weeks; she often admits that the family is so unpredictable that she never knows what she will find at any visit.

Janice and Jewel have attended the junior high school together for almost four months; during this time, they each have missed forty days of school. The principal, the social worker, and the superintendent were not able to get the girls to attend school more frequently than this. Pressure was placed upon the parents for the girls to attend; but with little or no effect; most of the teachers believed that putting pressure on the parents and the girls only made things worse. This is Jaylene's first year to attend the high school; academically, Jaylene never has been a strong student even when she occasionally studied. None of the girls have liked any of the classes in school and quite often did pranks so that they would be asked to leave school or would be suspended.

Jewel is seven months pregnant and attends special classes for expectant mothers three times a week; Jaylene is extremely jealous of Jewel because she wants to be pregnant, too. Janice dates a man who is thirty years old; the parents have made no comment on any of the experiences of the girls. When pressed for a reaction to Janice's dating an older man, the parents responded by saying, "She's going to do what she's going to do. There's nothing that we can do to stop her."

The mother works occasionally as a maid; the father is an alcoholic and works when he needs money. The parents never have taken any interest in the girls, their schoolwork, or social behaviors. The social worker has provided many hours of counseling and instruction to help the parents provide more supervision for the girls; however, nothing has seemed to work. The parents and the girls seem to do what they want to do when they want to do it. It is like observing two separate families living in one room together.

QUESTIONS

1. What are the problems? What changes must occur?
2. How can the curriculum be altered to meet the girls' special needs?
3. As the school counselor, how can you be of service to Jaylene?
4. How should the curriculum be altered to meet Jewel's special needs?
5. As the homeroom teacher, how could you provide assistance for these individuals?
6. How has the educational environment provided for the development of the girls' self-esteem and self-concept?

Case Study 51
Mrs. Kelly

Mrs. Kelly observes Kenneth from a distance as he struggles to write the first draft of a research paper for the fifth-period junior English class. She knows that it is not Kenneth's favorite or easiest subject. She remembers him from her freshman English class several years prior to this year. Mrs. Kelly has taught English at the school for almost ten years. She is well respected by her peers, the students, and the staff. Many regard her as a very good teacher and respect her opinion. Kenneth always has had difficulty with writing, especially writing the form and having the content in a composition that Mrs. Kelly expects. Mrs. Kelly suggests to him that if he will stay after school, she will help him work on his paper; she has offered her help many times. Kenneth has always had some reason not to accept her help. This time being no different, Kenneth tells her that he has to work and cannot stay after school. Mrs. Kelly tells him that he will have to make dramatic improvements in his work if he is to pass junior English. The exchange has not been good for either individual; they both leave believing that the other person had expected much too much.

Mrs. Kelly stands close to Craig as he works on the final draft of the paragraph; he has made tremendous progress in his writing since the first day of freshman English. She has been careful to encourage the members of the freshmen class; she wants them to experience success early in the writing process. Mrs. Kelly has observed that freshmen who have success early in the writing phase of the class experience success later. She has been careful to encourage respect for rather than fear or dread of the discipline. Craig appears to be one of her early success stories. Mrs. Kelly and Craig enjoy a cordial exchange during and after the class. Craig always has enjoyed classes, but especially Mrs. Kelly's class.

Craig, fifteen years old and in the ninth grade, and Kenneth, seventeen years old and in the eleventh grade, are brothers. They have attended the same small, rural, union school for almost five years. They have been described by their teachers as conscientious, hardworking, honest, and dependable students. They rarely miss school; it is unusual for the boys to be late for breakfast, lunch, or school. Many students and staff have kidded the boys that the only reason that they attend school is to eat. Only the principal, his secretary, and the cafeteria manager know the truth about the boys.

Craig and Kenneth are average students in the classroom. They find that participating in classroom activities to be of minor importance. Their parents abandoned them almost five years ago; even after almost five years, no one is able to locate the parents or know much about them. The family had moved to the area from a large nearby city; in the city, they had lived in an apartment in a public housing complex. They did not know, nor did they try to get to know, any of their neighbors. They had learned early that it was wise to be quiet and keep to themselves in the big city. They had tried to follow this policy while living in this school district also.

The family had lived together in a mobile home on property that they had bought after moving to the area. To the casual observer, everything appeared as a normal family living in a rural area. On the first day of September, their parents had gotten up early and left without telling the boys where they were going or when they would be returning. This was not unusual to the boys; their parents had often taken extended trips that had lasted for several months without telling them much about it. They were used to living by themselves and caring for themselves without benefit of adult supervision.

The boys worked at any odd jobs that they could find in the area; they worked at the school, the local fire department, or the local service station. The money that the boys earned had gone to pay for the taxes on the property, electricity, food, and clothing. No matter how hard that they had worked, they never seemed to be able to earn enough money.

The boys had been taught to be self-reliant and to keep quiet about the business of the family. The boys had friends only at school; they never had anyone to visit their home. At the beginning of this school year, money had been hard to make. The boys went to the principal and told him that their parents had to stay a rather long distance from the school district; therefore, they had no money for school, food, or school supplies. The principal had agreed with the boys to keep the information confidential; however, he did have his secretary work on locating clothing, food, and general supplies for the boys. For the past five years, no one at the school or in the local community knew that the boys had lived in a mobile home alone without any adult supervision or support.

QUESTIONS

1. How can Mrs. Kelly help Kenneth?
2. How can the curriculum be altered to be more helpful to Craig?

3. How can the school become involved with the boys?
4. How can social services and the school work together to help families similar to this one?
5. What should the principal do?

Case Study 52
Glenn

Glenn is almost ten years old; he is the only boy in a family of nine children. By birth position, he is the middle child. He lives in a situation that can only be described as a rural family struggling economically to survive. Being the only male child in the family, he has been given many adult chores and responsibilities. His youngest sister, Dawn, is three years old, Kathy is six, Meg seven, Karen eight, the twin girls eleven, Brenda twelve, and the oldest sister, Gail, thirteen; Gail has severe asthma that limits any physical activities. The twins, Faye and Maye, have been classified as being severely mentally handicapped; they have been in special education classes since the second grade.

From her perspective in the classroom, Mrs. Jackson describes Glenn as bright, personable, and having a magical sense of humor that all the children seem to enjoy. He is usually the center of all group games that are played in the fourth grade. Mrs. Jackson has assessed his academic efforts and finds that he is a superior student in all areas. Glenn is much more mature physically, socially, and emotionally than any of his peer group. When he attends school on a regular basis, academically he is at the top of his class.

Unfortunately, Glenn has had to miss a lot of days to do chores at home for his parents. Thus far into the school year, as Halloween is approaching, he has missed fifteen days. The parents have reported to the principal that he has had to do things at home rather than his being absent due to illness. They have explained consistently that they desperately need Glenn at home to help; they don't have any other person on whom to rely.

Glenn's problem is poverty. His family only has enough food and money to survive on a week-to-week basis. His father has tuberculosis and is not able to work; he requires weekly trips to the local medical clinic. His mother works at a local restaurant for minimum wage; she appears overwhelmed by everything that has occurred in the family. Money is the focus of all family life; there is never enough to cover all of the needs of the family beyond the basics—food and shelter. With so many people to provide for and with so many individuals who need extensive medical care, the family appears to be facing disaster from all sides. The family struggles to meet the immediate needs of the individual on an emergency basis.

Mrs. Jackson observed that Glenn had worn the same clothes to school during the first days of this school year that he had worn during the previous year. The clothing was much too small for his developing body. Much of what he had worn appeared to need laundering badly.

QUESTIONS

1. How can the school help Glenn? Should the school/school district attempt to provide assistance to Glenn? Should any other agency become involved?
2. How can Mrs. Jackson provide the necessary support and guidance for Glenn?
3. How should the curriculum be modified to address the individual needs of Glenn?
4. What sources within the classroom setting or outside of the school are available to help Glenn and his family?

UNIT 10
Homeless Students

Case Study 53
Jake and Jacob

Jake is thirteen and Jacob is fourteen; they live in any of the abandoned houses in the neighborhood. Although their parents are living in the neighborhood, the boys have lived on their own for the past three years. They have been very successful in avoiding all of the assistance programs directed by the school district, social services, and the community. For the past three weeks, the boys have been living in an abandoned house that is a known "crack house." The police report that the boys have been supporting themselves by stealing and dealing drugs throughout the community.

Mr. Shinn is the junior high science teacher. He teaches both Jake and Jacob in his science classes. Jake is in the second period seventh-grade science class, and Jacob is in the third period eighth-grade science class. The boys respect Mr. Shinn. They admire his knowledge of how things work. Mr. Shinn has been able to establish a positive relationship with the boys. They do listen to his suggestions and occasionally ask his opinion about many personal questions. However, they do not tell him everything; they tell him only what they want him to know.

In the classroom, both boys view education as a waste of time. They attend school only to make contacts for buying and selling drugs or to make money. When asked by the guidance counselor their view of education or the school, they respond that it is a place to make or "break" a deal. Although both of the boys are quite capable of being successful in academics, they choose not to be. They rarely submit any homework assignments to any of the teachers. The boys announce proudly that they are waiting for their sixteenth birthday, when they don't have to legally attend school.

They are viewed by their classmates with great suspicion. Mr. Shinn has stated that he does not believe that the boys have any friends at school. In the classroom, they are not rude to any of the teachers; teachers have described the boys as being very quiet and reserved. They do not stand out for anything they have done or said in the classroom.

When Mr. Shinn has tried to speak with the parents, they refuse to speak of the boys, or anything that has happened at the school. Mr. Shinn stated once that talking to the parents was one of the most frustrating experiences. They refuse to participate in any conversation that relates to the actions of the boys.

When the boys have been placed in any of the vocational classes, all of the teachers report that much of the equipment begins to disappear. During the past year, the boys have been caught numerous times trying to sell school equipment. The boys have tried to steal both small and large items. The vocational teacher says that the boys have taken the last four staplers that he has tried to provide for the class. They also have been caught trying to carry out the xerox machine from the vocational classroom.

The principal reports that working with social services, the courts, and any of the welfare agencies has been extremely frustrating. All indicate the need for something to be done about the boys; however, all indicate a large caseload and having little time to devote to dealing with boys that are not creating any large problems for the school or for the community.

QUESTIONS

1. How should Mr. Shinn plan for the boys in his science classes? Is there anything he can do to address the boys' needs?
2. What vocational education strategies would be appropriate for the boys?
3. What specific classroom adaptations would be necessary to meet the boys' needs?
4. Is a traditional classroom an ideal placement for the boys? Why? Why not?

Case Study 54
The Hawkes Family

The Hawkes are a family of three—a mother; Becky, who is nine; and Beth Ann, who is eleven. The girls and their mother live at the local homeless shelter. Jennifer Borz believes that the family has been in the community for almost six months living anywhere there is shelter and food.

Jennifer teaches a third-grade class at the elementary school. This is Mrs. Borz's fifth year teaching in the third grade. Many of the teachers in the school have acknowledged that Jennifer is a talented teacher who works hard to create a positive learning environment for her students. She has had Becky in her class for almost three weeks. The longest period of attendance for Becky or her sister is about three days. Jennifer does not believe that the family can live at any one place longer than four or five days.

The principal, the community, the school, and welfare agencies have been unsuccessful in providing a solution for the Hawkes. Mrs. Hawkes spends any money that she receives on alcohol, remains in a stupor for the length of the effects of the alcohol, and neglects the children. When the child welfare agency has removed the children, Becky and Beth Ann quickly return to their mother. Without their mother present, they are violent, combative, and non-cooperative. With their mother present, the girls respond to their mother's commands.

After having been physically attacked by both girls and their mother, Jennifer has learned when working with Becky to be very careful using words that would reflect negatively upon the mother. The attack had occurred during the second day that Becky and her sister had been enrolled in the school. It was after the school had been dismissed for the day. Jennifer Borz had been trying to find information about the condition of the family. Her curiosity was motivated by a genuine interest to help the family.

During an early afternoon reading session, Becky fretted over a writing assignment. Jennifer remained close to Becky, trying to reassure her. She remained inconsolable; nothing that Jennifer said to her made a difference. After several minutes of letting Becky struggle to resolve the problem, Jennifer sat down beside her and began to speak softly to her. Immediately, Becky began to shout at Jennifer, throw all of the writing materials around the classroom, and began to run about the classroom screaming.

During a conference with the principal, Jennifer learned that Beth Ann's teacher had a similar incident during the morning reading session. The teacher had received several bruises from Beth Ann following the rage. The teacher had the principal remove Beth Ann from the classroom and try to locate the mother for assistance.

QUESTIONS

1. How does Jennifer Borz regain control of the classroom environment?
2. What should she do first in dealing with Becky?
3. What would you recommend that Jennifer do in working with Becky?
4. Could there have been any warning signs that the teachers missed?

Case Study 55
Donna

Donna is twelve years old, and her mother is thirty years old but looks twenty years older. Years of having to live on the streets and work at various jobs to support herself and Donna have exacted a heavy toll. Currently, the family lives in a one-room shed attached to the rear of a liquor store about three blocks from the elementary school.

All of the students in the second grade are aware of the problems of Donna and her mother. They avoid Donna as much as they can. Mrs. Connors, the second-grade teacher, tries to involve Donna in all activities; some attempts are successful, but others are not. Donna reacts to the students' treatment with a shrug and tries to hide in her desk. It is a small community where everyone knows everyone. The community has not been helpful to Donna and her mother.

One day during the math class before lunch, Mrs. Connors places the students into groups to work on several problem-solving activities. She has reasoned that if the students learn that Donna has ability, they will accept her more readily. The students work for almost fifteen minutes. There are no unpleasant comments from the students in Donna's group, and Mrs. Connors begins to feel that the experiment has been successful. As she moves about the classroom observing class behavior, she stands near Donna's group and listens to the interaction between the students. She does not hear any negative comments from the group.

During the lunch period, Mrs. Connors asks the individual students how successful the math exercise was. She is surprised to hear from the students that they had hated having to work with Donna. They tell her that they are going to complain to their parents, the principal, and anyone who will listen to them about having to work with Donna. All the students in the second grade sit quietly during the lunch period. The principal notices the students' conduct and tries to talk them to individually. They repeat soberly what they said to Mrs. Connors. The principal realizes that there is a major problem, so she schedules a meeting with Mrs. Connors and several other school staff during the lunch period.

QUESTIONS

1. How can Mrs. Connors help Donna to become more accepted by the group?
2. What can Mrs. Connors do to help the students in her class to be more tolerant?
3. What activities should the second-grade teacher do to help Donna be able to work with various groups?
4. What should the principal address during the meeting?

Case Study 56
Jacob Is Sixteen Years Old

Jacob is a sixteen-years-old tenth-grader who struggles socially and academically. Schoolwork on his grade level is very difficult for him. He seldom finishes assignments on time. When Mrs. Graham asks him where his work is, he often insists to the point of tears that he handed the assignment in but someone must have taken it or she must have lost it. Other excuses have included: his sister lost it, or his mother made him go somewhere the night before, so he didn't have time to do any homework. Often Mrs. Graham finds the half-finished assignment stuffed in his desk, notebook, or a variety of books in his desk.

Jacob has no close friends of whom Mrs. Graham is aware. Some of the more easygoing students tolerate him but never choose to be around him. He often misses the morning break because of incomplete work. When he does get to have a break, he usually ends up in an argument over rules and unfair treatment from the other students. The others do often deliberately try to exclude him from games, discussion, or friendly teasing. Even if a teacher is nearby watching to ensure that everyone is conducting themselves in a proper manner, Jacob still claims he has been singled out for unfair treatment. He then often cries. He cries over minor rule infractions. During the lunch period, he tattles on other students not obeying the rules. He tattles by saying that the other students are calling him names and tormenting him. Sometimes they are, but more often they are totally unaware of his presence.

Jacob always want to sit by Mrs. Graham, assist her, or to be her partner. He tries to put his arm around her and sit very close, too close for her personal comfort. He depends on adults for their approval. He wants to be the one to run errands or do any small job in the classroom. He is often out of his seat asking to do these tasks when he should be in his seat working on the assignment. If Mrs. Graham sees Jacob outside of the school environment, he always gives her an enthusiastic greeting. Often he has crossed a very busy street just to say hello to her.

Jacob has a fourteen-year-old sister and a six-year-old brother. The sister is in the gifted program at the school. She has a domineering personality, which is attested to by all of her teachers. Jacob lives with his parents. His father farms and works at a second job; his mother is a teacher in another school district. A teacher who taught with Jacob's mother for several years expressed surprise upon discovering that there are two boys in Jacob's family. The teacher believed the daughter was an only child, because the mother spoke only of her.

At parent–teacher conferences, the mother always expressed the feeling that Jacob could do the work, but just didn't have the confidence. She placed the blame on a first-grade teacher who wanted Jacob to repeat the first grade. The mother felt that the teacher "ruined" Jacob because of this negative attitude.

The mother occasionally sent notes to school indicating that Jacob should bring his work home, so she would be able to help him. However, every afternoon, the work goes home with Jacob only to be returned the following day untouched.

When Jacob is asked how he feels about school and learning, he says in a most emphatic tone that he likes school, but he doesn't like to do the work. He seldom misses school. He has been present even when he actually wasn't feeling well enough to have been in school. From the homeroom teacher's perspective, Jacob should have been home in bed.

QUESTIONS

1. What factors to indicate that Jacob may be considered "at risk?"
2. Can it be assumed that Jacob will continue in this pattern of behavior? Why? Why not?
3. What is the problem in this case? Describe some of the characteristics.
4. What is Jacob's current level of functioning in the classroom environment?

Selected Theorists and Their Theories

ALBERT BANDURA (1925–PRESENT): SOCIAL LEARNING THEORY—BEHAVIORISM

SELECTED FEATURES

- Patterns of behavior are learned through observation.
- Using verbal/imagined symbols, experiences can be preserved for guiding anticipated further behavior.
- Should be able to control behavior through arranging environmental consequences and/or cognitive supports.

EFFECTS OF OBSERVATION

- Can acquire new responses that did not previously exist.
- Can strengthen/weaken responses—positive/negative.
- Can serve as a platform for demonstration of learned responses—short/long term.

MODEL REINFORCED

- One demonstrating high status/prestige from the observer's perspective.
- One controlling rewards or is rewarded for single event/behavior.
- One perceived as a peer—similar age, sex, intelligence, social status, sphere of influence.

IMITATION OF BEHAVIOR

- Behavior has not been reinforced; individual lacks self-efficacy or self-esteem.
- Individual lacks the competence to model behavior.
- Behavior has been reinforced for matching idealized response.
- Individual is independent of environmental influences.
- Behavior is observed as being a model to perceived self-concept or self-image.

DEMONSTRATION OF CONSEQUENCE OF BEHAVIOR

- Clearly identify appropriate behavior/response.
- Clearly identify appropriate time/place/event for behavior/response.
- Motivation is necessary to imitate/not imitate a behavior.

Continued

ALBERT BANDURA *continued*

MODELING

- Observe effect of model being imitated.
- Identify code(s) and symbols reflected.
- Individual can reproduce behavior.
- Positively / negatively reinforce behavior.

Adapted from Bandura, A. (1969). *Social learning and personality development.*
New York: Holt, Rinehart & Winston.

JEROME SEYMOUR BRUNER (1915–PRESENT): THEORY OF MOTIVATION

FIRST PRINCIPLE—MOTIVATION

Specifies conditions that predispose the individual to learn. Students have an "in-built curiosity to learn"—intrinsic motivation; he holds that reciprocity, "a need to work cooperatively with others," is a form of extrinsic motivation (activation—need of uncertainty to motivate; maintenance—exploration needs to be encouraged; direction—knowledge of goal/relevance of task performed to the achievement of goal).

SECOND PRINCIPLE—STRUCTURE

Bruner holds that any given subject area, any body of knowledge, can be organized in some optimal fashion so that it can be transmitted/understood by almost any student (mode of presentation: enactive representation—expression in terms of actions; iconic representation—thinking when objects become conceivable without actions; symbolic representation—translating experiences into language).

THIRD PRINCIPLE—SEQUENCE

The extent to which a student encounters difficulty in mastering a given subject depends upon the sequence of the material presented. Teaching involves leading the learner through a sequence of the various aspects of the subject. Intellectual development occurs from innately sequential movement from enactive through iconic to symbolic representation; Bruner believed this to be the best sequence for any subject. Teacher should begin with wordless messages, speaking mainly to the student's muscular responses. Student should be encouraged to develop graphs/charts/diagrams to assimilate the material. Instruction should occur symbolically through use of words.

FOURTH PRINCIPLE—REINFORCEMENT

Learning requires reinforcement. It is necessary to receive feedback about how we are doing; timing is critical to success in learning. Results must be learned at the time a student is evaluating their own performance. The instructor's role is crucial for success of the individual learner.

Continued

JEROME SEYMOUR BRUNER *continued*

DISCOVERY LEARNING

Bruner held that discovery learning is the only *acceptable* form of learning. Through insightful questioning and prompting by the teacher, students discover for themselves some of the basic principles. Learning through carefully arranged tasks by the teacher leads the student to discoveries that enable him or her to reach a level of understanding that surpasses the rote memorization of unrelated facts.

Adapted from Bruner, J. S. (1962). *The process of education.* Cambridge, MA: Harvard University Press.

ERIK HOMBURGER ERIKSON (1902–1994): STAGES OF PSYCHOSOCIAL DEVELOPMENT

0–2 YEARS: TRUST VS. MISTRUST

A child learns trust if the maternal/paternal individ_____ the infant's needs consistently and affectionately. Di_____ mother/father is inconsistent, negative, or n_____.

2–3 YEARS: AUTONOMY VS. SHAME ____ DOUBT

A child learns trust if the maternal/patern___ individual meets the infant's needs consistently and affectio_____ Distrust is learned if the mother/father is inconsistent, n_____, or neglectful.

3–6 YEARS: INITIATIVE ___ GUILT

Children utilize language/develop physical sk____ to explore/master environment around them, developing a sense of ____ initiative. If they encounter conflict with others/become frightened, or ___ are made to feel their ideas and/or activities are insignificant, guilt will ____op.

6–12 YEARS: INDUSTRY VS. INFERIORITY

Industry develops when children master tasks, complete objectives, and are recognized for achievements. They feel inferior if they fail often, are compared with peers negatively, or are not recognized for their activities/accomplishments.

12–18 YEARS: IDENTITY VS. ROLE CONFUSION/ IDENTITY DIFFUSION

Identity is achieved when one finds inner uniformity/wholeness/completeness and can address the question, "Who am I?" If one is unable to select from roles and value systems, or loses an identity by overidentification with others, role confusion/identity diffusion results.

18–35: YOUNG ADULTHOOD—INTIMACY VS. ISOLATION

One who has the ability to maintain an identity while sharing self with another has achieved intimacy. Isolation occurs when one competes/is combative with others rather than sharing total intimacy.

Continued

ERIK HOMBURGER ERIKSON *continued*

35–55: MIDDLE AGE ADULTHOOD GENERATIVITY VS. SELF-ABSORPTION OR STAGNATION

An individual concerning self with aiding/nurturing the next generation/producing meaningful work as an extension of self is experiencing generativity. One who is unable/incapable of helping others/is self-absorbed becomes stagnated.

BEYOND 55: LATE ADULTHOOD—INTEGRITY VS. DESPAIR

When one is able to look back over one's life and review it favorably, a sense of integrity is felt. If one feels that one's life has been without merit and it is now too late to make up for past errors/mistakes/lost opportunities, despair results.

Adapted from Erikson, E. (1963). *Childhood and society* (2nd ed.). New York: Norton; Erikson, E. (1968). *Identity, youth, and crises*. New York: Norton.

LAWRENCE KOHLBERG (1927–1987): THEORY OF MORAL DEVELOPMENT

PRECONVENTIONAL LEVEL

Behavior is determined by outside forces.
Judgment is based on personal needs and others' rules.

Stage 1: Punishment and Obedience Orientation

A child learns trust if the maternal/paternal individual meets the infant's needs consistently and affectionately. Distrust is learned if the mother/father is inconsistent, negative, or neglectful.

Stage 2: Personal Reward Orientation

A child learns trust if the maternal/paternal individual meets the infant's needs consistently and affectionately. Distrust is learned if the mother/father is inconsistent, negative, or neglectful.

CONVENTIONAL LEVEL

Behavior is concerned with good acts/maintaining social order. Judgment is based on others' approval, family expectations, traditional values, the laws of society, and loyalty to country.

Stage 3: Punishment and Obedience Orientation

A child learns trust if the maternal/paternal individual meets the infant's needs consistently and affectionately. Distrust is learned if the mother/father is inconsistent, negative, or neglectful.

Stage 4: Personal Reward Orientation

A child learns trust if the maternal/paternal individual meets the infant's needs consistently and affectionately. Distrust is learned if the mother/father is inconsistent, negative, or neglectful.

Continued

LAWRENCE KOHLBERG *continued*

POSTCONVENTIONAL LEVEL

Behavior is focused on self-accepted moral principles.

Stage 5: Punishment and Obedience Orientation

A child learns trust if the maternal/paternal individual meets the infant's needs consistently and affectionately. Distrust is learned if the mother/father is inconsistent, negative, or neglectful.

Stage 6: Personal Reward Orientation

A child learns trust if the maternal/paternal individual meets the infant's needs consistently and affectionately. Distrust is learned if the mother/father is inconsistent, negative, or neglectful.

Adapted from Kohlberg, L. (1975). The cognitive-developmental approach to moral education. *Phi Delta Kappan, 56,* 670–677.

ABRAHAM HAROLD MASLOW (1908–1970): THEORY OF MOTIVATION

HIERARCHY OF NEEDS

The lowest/most basic needs must be satisfied to some extent before the higher level of needs can be considered. If an individual loses the lowest level of needs, the hierarchy of needs reverts to that most basic level of needs before progressing to the higher level.

BASIC THEORY

Physiological Needs: Food, drink, sex, shelter

Safety Needs: Order, security, protection, and family stability

Love Needs: Affection, group affiliation, and personal acceptance

Esteem Needs: Self-efficacy, self-esteem, prestige, reputation, and social status

Self-Actualization Needs: Self-fulfillment and achievement of personal goals, ambitions, and talent

CONCEPTS

Hierarchy of Needs: The lowest/most basic needs must be satisfied to some extent before the higher-level needs can be considered.

Self-Actualization: Becoming the very best that one can become; fulfillment of one's anticipated potential/capacity

Inner Nature: Consideration of one's most basal biological abilities that guide the development and growth

Deficiency of Needs: Lower four levels of needs focus individual on the fulfillment, which would lead to completion, to a stronger desire for fulfillment.

Growth Needs: Self-actualizing needs in which the individual has a desire/need to know/to understand him- or herself; the direction to understand the environment and the individual's relationship to that environment; a desire for esthetic experiences/feelings of completion within the universe

Adapted from Maslow, A. (1970). *Motivation and personality.* New York: Harper & Row.

JEAN PIAGET (1896–1980): THEORY OF COGNITIVE DEVELOPMENT

BIRTH TO 2 YEARS: SENSORIMOTOR

- Transition from completely overlearning to internal thought (use of senses, reflexes, and motoric manipulations)
- Object permanence
- Differentiate self from environment
- Primitive understanding of time, space, and causations
- Development of mean / end relationship
- Imitation (from simple to complex)

2–7 YEARS: PREOPERATIONAL

- Able to use symbols (language), symbolic play, and internal thought
- Egocentric (view of world from own point of view)
- Thinking unsystematic / illogical (transductive reasoning– from random item to item)
- Centers on one aspect of object / problem at a time
- Cannot reverse processes but has rudiments of conservation and classification
- Does not have a structure of whole, but rather many isolated fragments

7–11 YEARS: CONCRETE OPERATIONS

- Can conserve mass, length, weight, and volume
- Able to reverse and decenter
- Classification (organize objects into an organized schema)
- Seriation (order of objects into ordered series / parts)
- Logical thinking based on direct experiences / identifiable objects that can be imagined

11–12 YEARS: FORMAL OPERATIONS

- Hypothetical / deductive reasoning (can identify possible solutions to problem solving, can test systematically)
- Inductive reasoning (can move from specific facts to formulate general principles and conclusions)

Continued

JEAN PIAGET *continued*

- Reflective abstractions (can reflect on self / what might happen)
- Able to reason in purely symbolic / abstract manner

TERMS

Organization—ongoing process of arranging information / experiences into meaningful patterns

Adaptation—adjustment to the environment

Scheme—mental system or category of perception / experiences

Assimilation—fitting new information into existing schemes

Accommodation—altering existing schemes, or creating new ones in response to new information

Equilibration—search for mental balance between cognitive / information from environment

Disequilibrium—"out of balance" state that occurs when a person realizes current scheme is not appropriate in examining a current problem

Operation—actions a person carries out by thinking them through instead of performing them

Adapted from Piaget, J. (1952). *The origins of intelligence in children* (M. Cook, Trans.). New York: International University Press.

Carl Rogers (1902–1987): Hierarchy of Needs of Human Motivation

Needs		Physiological and Psychological Indicators
	LEVEL 7	
Actualization		Development to one's fullest capacity
	LEVEL 6	
Enhancement		Positive experiences and movement toward growth
	LEVEL 5	
Congruency		Real needs of self in relation o the perceived needs of self
	LEVEL 4	
Positive Regard		Value placed upon one for oneself, regardless of the specific behavior
	LEVEL 3	
Self-Worth		Need for individual to believe in own self-worth and dignity; to adhere to certain standards
	LEVEL 2	
Self-Awareness		Sensory and visceral awareness; awareness of self as well as environment
	LEVEL 1	
Maintenance		Basic biological needs: taste, sleep, hunger, thirst, smell, touch

Adapted from Rogers, C. (1969). *Freedom to learn.* Columbus, OH: Charles E. Merrill.

LEV SEMIONOVICH VYGOTSKY (1896–1934): THEORY OF INSTRUCTION

Higher order cognitive processes are the essential building block for logical thought, comprehension, and generalization.

Vygotsky emphasized the value of interaction (group work); he neither would claim that we learn exclusively either alone or with others.

INSTRUCTIONAL PRINCIPLES

1. Effective teaching precedes curricular development stage of the learner.
2. Child is an active participant in the learning process, not a passive receiver.
3. Education includes a major social interactive component with parents, teachers, and peers. Effective learning occurs with an active reflection with adults, parents, and peers.
4. Stages of cognition are a series of significantly reorganized systems that undergo a systemic restructuring and reorganization.
5. Each stage of cognitive development is qualitative. The transitions involve disintegration prior to new and more complex integration. No growth occurs without significant interactions.
6. The cerebral cortex undergoes neurological reorganization during stage growth. (See also cell-assembly concepts in Hebb, D. O. [1949]. *The organization of behavior.* New York: Wiley.)

ZONE OF PROXIMAL DEVELOPMENT

Conceptual space, or zone between what children are capable of doing on their own and what they can achieve with assistance from an adult, or more capable peer. The term implies a sense of readiness—(1) when child is prepared to undertake a task, the child can move to a qualitatively different level using a process called "scaffolding." The scaffold enables the student to move sequentially through a complex task using each of the steps / stages to secure the information concretely before moving to the next level.

Adapted from Vygotsky, L. S. (1993). *The collected works of L. S. Vygotsky: Vol 2* (J. Knox & C. Stevens, Trans.). New York: Plenum Press.

Additional Resources

CASE STUDY: A REVIEW FORMAT

Case Study _____

Name _____ **Date** _____

I. Statement of the Problem.

II. Learning Theories Applicable to the Case.

III. Suggested Teaching Strategies.

IV. Responses to Questions in the Case Study.

Learning Assessment

Name _____ Date _____

Assessment Instrument	Characteristics from Assessment
Gregorc Learning Styles (Antony Gregorc)	List characteristics that approximate your identified style of learning List any comments appropriate to your style of learning
Dunn & Dunn Learning Styles (Rita and Kenneth Dunn)	List characteristics that approximate your identified style of learning List any comments appropriate to your style of learning
Myers-Briggs	List characteristics that approximate your identified style of learning List any comments appropriate to your style of learning
Learning Styles Inventory	List characteristics that approximate your identified style of learning List any comments appropriate to your style of learning

How do I learn?

Suggestions for writing this section:

- Write this in one or two paragraphs.
- Examine the characteristics from all of the assessment instruments.
- Determine common items in all of them.
- Determine strength and weakness identified by the instruments.
- Select two or three characteristics to focus writing.
- Provide an "overall" picture of how you approach learning.

Constructivism

VYGOTSKY'S FOUR BASIC CONCEPTS OF CONSTRUCTIVISM

1. Children CONSTRUCT knowledge.
2. Learning can LEAD development.
3. Development cannot be separated from its SOCIAL CONTEXT.
4. Language plays a central role in MENTAL DEVELOPMENT.

DEFINITION OF CONSTRUCTIVISM

Constructivism is defined in the *Dictionary of Psychology* (Reber, 1995) as

> A general theoretical position that characterizes perception and perceptual experience as being constructed from, in Gregory's words, "fleeting fragmentary scraps of data signaled by the senses and drawn from the brain's memory banks."

> The essence of all constructivist theories is that perceptual experience is viewed as more than a direct response to stimulation. It is viewed as an elaboration or "construction" based on hypothesized cognitive and affective operation.

TYPES OF CONSTRUCTIVISM

There are three types of constructivism (Woolfolk, 1999, pp. 277–278):

> Exogenous Constructivism: "Focuses on the ways that individuals reconstruct outside reality by building accurate mental representations (e.g., propositional networks, schemas, and condition-action production rules)." Learning is building accurate mental structures that reflect the way

things really are in the world. Many aspects of information processing are consistent with exogenous constructivism.

Endogenous Constructivism: "Assumes that new knowledge is abstracted from old knowledge and is not shaped by accurately mapping the outside world. Knowledge develops as old cognitive structures are transformed to become more coordinated and useful." Piaget's stage theory of cognitive development is an example of endogenous constructivism.

Dialectical Constructivism: "Suggests that knowledge grows through the interactions of internal (cognitive) and external (environmental and social) factors." Vygotsky's description of cognitive development through the internalization and use of cultural tools such as language is an example of dialectical constructivism.

THE FOUR CORNERSTONES OF EMOTIONAL INTELLIGENCE

First Cornerstone: Emotional Literacy

  1. Emotional Honesty
  2. Emotional Energy
  3. Emotional Feedback
  4. Emotional Honesty

Second Cornerstone: Emotional Fitness

  5. Authentic Presence
  6. Trust Radius
  7. Constructive Discontent
  8. Resilience and Renewal

Third Cornerstone: Emotional Depth

  9. Unique Potential and Purpose
  10. Commitment, Accountability, and Conscience
  11. Applied Integrity
  12. Influence without Authority

Fourth Cornerstone: Emotional Alchemy

  13. Intuitive Flow
  14. Reflective Time-Shifting
  15. Opportunity Sensing
  16. Creating the Future

Cooper, Robert K., and Sawaf, Ayman. (1997). *Executive EQ: Emotional Intelligence in Leadership & Organizations*. New York: Grosset/Putnam.

TASKS TO ENCOURAGE STUDENTS TO USE KNOWLEDGE MEANINGFULLY

1. Decision Making

2. Investigation
   definitional (what)
   historical (how / why)
   projective (if . . . then)

3. Experimental Inquiry
   observe
   analyze
   predict (explain why)
   test prediction

4. Problem Solving
   structured (one answer)
   unstructured ([1] real life; [2] academic)

5. Invention
   the process of creating something new to meet a
   perceived need

Characteristics of Adolescents

Interested in experimenting	Must be part of a "clique"	Act according to the approval of others	Feel the need for a relationship	Their WANTS outweigh their NEEDS
Identity search	Sexual experimentation	Goal search	Need peer/social skills	Strive for independence
Socialization	Self-esteem	Relevant skills	Identity	Decision-making skills
Healthy lifestyle	Accountability for ethical/moral values	Social/academic critical thinking and problem solving	Support ideas with specific examples	Social skills and communication skills
Peers are most important	Must find success to continue	Personal fable	Role playing	Moral judgments revolve around self-interests

This table was developed from a discussion in an educational psychology class conducted at Wayne State College by the author. "Adolescent" was defined as an individual between 13 and 19 years of age.

References

Airasian, P. W. (1994). *Classroom assessment* (2nd ed.). New York: McGraw-Hill.

Bandura, A. (1981). Cultivating competence, self-efficacy, and intrinsic interest through proximal self-motivation. *Journal of Personality and Social Psychology, 41,* 586–598.

Bandura, A. (1986). *Social foundations of thought and action.* Englewood Cliffs, NJ: Prentice-Hall.

Biehler, R. F., & Snowman, J. (1990). *Psychology applied to teaching* (6th ed.). Boston: Houghton Mifflin.

Brophy, J. (1992). Probing the subtleties of subject-matter teaching. *Educational Leadership, 49*(7), 4–8.

Bruer, J. T. (1993). Schools for thought: A science of learning in the classroom. Cambridge, MA: MIT Press.

Bruner, J. S. (1962). *The process of education.* Cambridge, MA: Harvard University Press.

Bruner, J. S. (1966). *Toward a theory of instruction.* Cambridge, MA: Harvard University Press.

Bruner, J. S. (1983). *Child's talk.* New York: Norton.

Bruner, J. S. (1987). *Actual minds, possible worlds.* Cambridge, MA: Harvard University Press.

Bruner, J. S. (1991). *Acts of meaning.* Cambridge, MA: Harvard University Press.

Cangelosi, J. S. (1990). *Cooperation in the classroom: Students and teachers together* (2nd ed.). Washington, DC: National Education Association.

Comer, J. P., Haynes, N. M., Joyner, E. T., & Ben-Avie, M. (Eds.). (1996). *Rallying the whole village: The Comer process for reforming education.* New York: Teachers College Press.

Elkind, D. (1986). *The miseducation children: Superkids at risk.* New York: Knopf.

Erikson, E. (1968). *Childhood and society* (2nd ed.). New York: Norton.

Erikson, E. (1980). *Identity, youth, and crisis.* New York: Norton.

Erikson, E. (1985). *Identity and the life cycle* (2nd ed.). New York: Norton.

Flavell, J. H. (1985). *The conditions of learning and theory of instruction* (4th ed.). Englewood Cliffs, NJ: Prentice-Hall.

Gagne, R. M. (1985). *The conditions of learning and theory of instruction* (4th ed.). New York: Holt, Rinehart & Winston.

Gardner, H. (1979). Developmental psychology after Piaget: An approach in terms of symbolization. *Human Development, 15,* 570–580.

Gardner, H. (1983). *Frames of mind.* New York: Basic Books.

Glasser, W. (1969). *Schools without failure.* New York: Harper & Row.

Glasser, W. (1990). *The quality school.* New York: Harper & Row.

Good, T. L., & Brophy, J. E. (1991). *Looking in the classrooms* (5th ed.). New York: HarperCollins.

Guilford, J. P. (1967). *The nature of human intelligence.* New York: McGraw-Hill.

Hebb, D. O. (1949). *The organization of behavior.* New York: Wiley.

Hunter, M. (1982). *Mastery teaching.* El Segundo, CA: TIP Publications.

Johnson, D. W., Johnson, R. T., & Holubec, E. J. (1994). *The new circles of learning: Cooperation in the classroom and school.* Alexandria, VA: Association for Supervision and Curriculum Development.

Kohlberg, L. (1975). The cognitive-developmental approach to moral education. *Phi Delta Kappan, 56,* 670–677.

Kohlberg, L. (1981). *Essays on moral development, Volume 1: The philosophy of moral development.* New York: Harper & Row.

Kounin, J. S. (1997). *Discipline and group management in classrooms.* New York: Holt, Rinehart & Winston.

Kowalski, T. J., Weaver, R. A., & Henson, K. T. (1990). *Case studies on teaching.* White Plains, NY: Longman.

Maslow, A. H. (1968). *Motivation and personality.* New York: D. Van Nostrand.

Perkins, D. N. (1986). *Knowledge as design.* Hillsdale, NJ: Lawrence Erlbaum Associates.

Piaget, J. (1962). *Comments on Vygotsky's critical remarks* (A. Parsons, Trans.). Cambridge, MA: MIT Press. (Original work published in 1934)

Piaget, J. (1978). *Success and understanding.* Cambridge, MA: Harvard University Press.

Piaget, J. (1995). *The language and thought of the child* (M. Gabain, Trans.). New York: Meridian. (Original work published in 1923)

Reber, A. R. (1995). *The dictionary of psychology.* New York: Penguin.

Rogers, C. R. (1969). *Freedom to learn.* Columbus, OH: Charles E. Merrill.

Rogers, C. R., & Freiberg, H. J. (1994). *Freedom to learn* (3rd ed.). Columbus, OH: Charles E. Merrill.

Sadker, M., Sadker, D., & Klein, S. (1991). The issue of gender in elementary and secondary education. *Review of Research in Education, 17,* 309–315.

Silverman, R., Welty, W. M., & Lyon, S. (1992). *Case studies for teacher problem solving.* New York: McGraw-Hill.

Skinner, B. F. (1953). *Science and human behavior.* New York: Macmillan.

Skinner, B. F. (1971). *Beyond freedom and dignity.* New York: Knopf.

Slavin, R. E. (1991). Are cooperative learning and "untracking" harmful to the gifted? *Educational Leadership, 48*(6), 68–71.

Slavin, R. E., Karweit, N. L., & Wasik, B. A. (December 1992 / January 1993). Preventing early school failure: What works. *Educational Leadership,* 10–18.

Slavin, R. E., Karweit, N. L., & Wasik, B. A. (1994). *Preventing early school failure.* Boston: Allyn & Bacon.

Sprinthall, R. C., Sprinthall, N. A., & Oja, S. N. (1998). *Educational psychology: A developmental approach* (7th ed.). Boston: McGraw-Hill.

Sternberg, R. J. (1983). *Handbook on human intelligence.* New York: Cambridge University Press.

Sternberg, R. J. (1985). *Beyond IQ.* New York: Cambridge University Press.

Teaching for multiple intelligences. (September 1997). *Educational Leadership, 55*(1), 1–111.

Telecommunications and new learning paradigms. (November/December 1999). *Syllabus, 13*(4), 1–62.

Terman, L. M. (1916). *The measurement of intelligence.* Boston: Houghton Mifflin.

Thorndike, E. L. (1913). Educational psychology. In *The psychology of learning .* New York: Teachers College Press.

Vygotsky, L. S. (1978). *Mind in society.* Cambridge: Harvard University Press.

Vygotsky, L. S. (1986). *Thought and language.* Cambridge: MIT Press.

Vygotsky, L. S. (1987). *Problems of general psychology.* New York: Plenum.

Vygotsky, L. S. (1993). *The collected works of L. S. Vygotsky* (Vol. 2) (J. Knox & C. Stevens, Trans.). New York: Plenum.

Walberg, H. J. (1990). Productive teaching and instruction: Assessing the knowledge base. *Phi Delta Kappan, 72,* 470–478.

Woolfolk, A. E. (1998). *Educational psychology* (7th ed.). Boston: Allyn & Bacon.

Zimmerman, B. J., & Schunk, D. H. (Eds.). (1989). *Self-regulated learning and academic achievement: Theory, research, and practice.* New York: Springer-Verlag.